PRAISE FOR

GETTING YOU READY FOR POWER

"Alexis pours her heart and life experiences into this book. It's a powerful guide for young women and girls who are ready to break past limiting beliefs, aim higher, seek out mentors, and step boldly into their power."

—**NELY GALÁN**, *New York Times* Bestselling Author of *Self Made: Becoming Empowered, Self-Reliant, and Rich in Every Way*

"A timely, empowering guide for women ready to move beyond self-doubt and into rooms where decisions, influence, and impact are made."

—**COURTNEY SPRITZER**, co-founder of Entreprenistas

"Alexis is doing important work to empower women to embrace leadership, confidence, and self-worth. I appreciate the meaningful conversations her book sparks about women stepping into their power and pursuing their goals."

—**AMINA ALTAI**, executive coach, speaker, and *USA Today* Bestselling Author of *The Ambition Trap*

"Alexis's book is a must-read for young girls, women, and allies of inclusion. Finding your authentic voice and confidence is vital for all. Alexis's message is inspiring, empowering, and uplifting. This book will not only help to elevate your professional career, but also elevate the case for inclusion and opportunity. The numbers are there, and the moment is now."

—**CID WILSON,** president & CEO, Hispanic Association on Corporate Responsibility (HACR)

GETTING YOU READY FOR POWER

A Woman's Guide to Building Confidence, Community, and Career Success

ALEXIS MERUELO

Published by Wonderwell Press
Austin, Texas
www.gbgpress.com

Distributed by River Grove Books

Design and composition by Greenleaf Book Group and Sheila Parr
Cover design by Greenleaf Book Group and Sheila Parr

Publisher's Cataloging-in-Publication data is available.

Print ISBN: 978-1-963827-40-8

eBook ISBN: 978-1-963827-41-5

First Edition

CONTENTS

INTRODUCTION

STARTING FROM WITHIN

Why do we crave and sometimes even feel addicted to the idea of being in a relationship? Humans have chased this feeling for centuries. People have crossed oceans and countries to find it, to secure it, and to hold on to it forever. And yet the single most important relationship we will ever have is the one we cultivate with ourselves.

I'll be the first to admit that I, too, was guilty of this endless pursuit. As you'll read in later chapters, I spent years searching for that "magical relationship." The one that would unlock all the answers to my unknowns. But eventually, I discovered that the person I had been waiting for all along was me. I was the one who needed to book the therapy appointments. I was the one who had to look back, dig deep, and face what was truly holding me back. And I was the one responsible for soul-searching and uncovering what truly sets my heart on fire.

So what is it that we're all really seeking? Is it love? A dream job? That idyllic beach house that looks like something out of a Nancy Meyers film? The truth is that each of us longs for something different. But here's what I've learned: You and only you are the answer to whatever it is you're searching for. And the secret ingredients? Love and belief in yourself. That is where everything begins.

Now, you may be wondering how this revelation came to me. I wish I could tell you it arrived easily, like a sudden wave of clarity. But the truth is that it didn't. It came through setbacks, struggles, and uncomfortable lessons. And yet it was one of those very setbacks that set the first domino in motion, one that I would like to share with you now.

Carl was a successful tech entrepreneur who sat on corporate boards with influence. By chance, our paths crossed through a mutual friend, and I felt he was a great person I could learn from. He took me under his wing and became someone whose opinion I respected. After a few months of working on new projects, I had an idea. I wanted to create an event for women to provide them with the resources, tools, and support to get into power. I wanted to meet women exactly where they were at and help them feel like they had the ability to become powerful, whatever that looked like to them. The more I thought about it, the more it became a dream of mine. I couldn't think about anything else for weeks. Plans poured out of me, and I scribbled them on napkins and scraps of paper. It was as if the universe were directing me to my next step—all the signs and support were there.

I finally got the courage to share my idea with Carl. But the moment I did, he shut it down. Instead of being supportive, he said it would be a big failure. "You'll have a hard time getting women to show up," he told me. "The event won't be big enough, and it will be detrimental to your brand and to the women I know if they participate. Don't bother wasting your time on something so small."

I was stunned. I sat there in silence for a while just trying to make sense of what he had said, but I couldn't. I waited until I got into the car to let the tears stream down my face as the images of the beautiful event I'd imagined turned from bright colors to gray. Worst of all? I went home that night and questioned my abilities, as was often my pattern. I felt my confidence drain right out of me as I replayed his words in my head. By the end of the week, whatever self-worth I had mustered up to that point in my life had disappeared.

But what I couldn't wrap my head around was how I could fail by trying to put on an event to inspire women. I couldn't accept his belief as truth. Something deep inside me roared back like a fire, and in that moment, everything changed.

They say the universe will test you once you've found your true calling, and that experience rocked me to my core. Defining moments like these can make us stronger on the road to the person we're becoming. As I look back on that day, I now see it as invaluable because it helped me truly solidify my purpose: to help women believe in themselves. And the more I have leaned into my passion, the more Carl's words have faded into the distance. I know he was put in my path for a reason. And he's just one of many who have tested my resolve, as I'm sure many of you have also experienced in your lives.

Today, I'm crystal clear: I will give my all to *any* opportunity to inspire and mentor young women to believe in themselves, no matter how many show up. *Every girl and woman matters.* Our words matter. Our stories matter. Our lessons matter. Our hearts matter. Our energies matter. And each of us has gifts to bring to the world that only we can bring, that only *women* can bring.

One of the topics we discuss as you continue reading is that women can be successful in business—the female way. We don't have to emulate men to excel. Empathy, warmth, caring, vulnerability, and cooperation are all needed, especially in business, now more than ever. The more I've worked in businesses across different industries, the more I've come to realize that these traits are our superpowers. They create strong and courageous leaders who encourage their team members to see them as empathetic and who see their team members as human beings.

My perspective at work has always been heart-driven. When I look at an issue within a business, my first question is whether every person in the situation is okay. Some see this as "weak." But in reality, putting people first is how you create a sustainable working environment where people feel valued and where employee retention is high. In fact, *Forbes* has reported: "According to research linking character strength with business performance, CEOs who score highly for traits like compassion and integrity can earn a 9.35% return on assets over two years."[1]

Not only do female leaders improve the quality of company culture, but they also increase the bottom line:

- Female-led S&P 500 companies outperformed male-led firms in ten-year returns, and the difference was significant—384 percent from female-led companies versus 261 percent from male-led companies.[2]
- Female CEOs and CFOs of Russell 3000 index companies generated $1.8 trillion more versus sector averages.[3]
- Firms with more women on their boards outperform those with mostly men.[4]

I want all women, and especially female Latinas like me, to embrace our feminine qualities and prove to ourselves that we *can* be successful in business while staying authentic. That we *can* be successful without losing our true voice or falling prey to the "machismo culture" so many of us endure. That we *can* be successful by embracing our qualities without being pressured into becoming aggressive or cutthroat. There is room for all of us. We deserve to sit at tables in every industry and present ourselves truthfully without wearing a false mask every day.

The more honest and real we are as leaders, the more the next generation of girls can see themselves as leaders without having to hide who they truly are. The more of us there are in leadership positions, the better companies will be positioned to make the best decisions collectively for society. And I'm on a quest to get more of us into leadership positions and help each of you believe you belong there.

But in order to get there, we have to work toward changing what we believe about ourselves. We have to rewire our negative thinking and free ourselves of the limitations that hold us back from reaching our full potential. We have to free ourselves to inspire more women to hold positions of power and be part of the collective change we seek. And to reach these goals, we have to start from within.

Success Is an Inside Job

As women, and especially those of us in marginalized groups, we can't count on the societal constructs that have been written for us. We have to write our own. Regardless of the obstacles of our societal constructs, each of us has the power to heal our past traumas and turn them into something powerful: *our passion.* But doing that is an inside job.

I know what it's like to hate yourself for twenty years. When I started working, I knew something was off. When I started dating, I knew something was off. When I started new projects, I knew something was off. There were so many moments when internally I knew something was not right with me. I was off-center and unaligned with my true self. My journey to confidence and self-worth wasn't perfect. There were ups, downs, pain, and heartbreak. But it's in these stories that I hope you find a piece of yourself, where you can relate to that embarrassing moment or gut-wrenching heartbreak. It's vulnerable and real. I won't sugarcoat the pain, and it's because I want you to know that I'm not perfect.

But after that incident with Carl, I knew I had reached my breaking point, and from that moment on, I vowed to spend the time and energy in healing and rebuilding myself. I committed to self-development and deep inner work that pushed me out of my comfort zone. I tried holistic therapies, I journaled, and I did guided meditations. I participated in retreats, and I read books by experts like Gabrielle Bernstein and Rachel Hollis. I put myself in rooms with other women where I didn't know a single person but took a leap of faith in knowing that we were all on the same mission. When I saw the growth play out in real time, I became obsessed and wanted to know everything there was about self-help. I immersed myself in all sorts of healing modalities.

In the process, I learned deep truths about myself, my

history, and women in this world. I became acquainted with the true core of who I am and what I want to bring. Out of all of this, a new version of myself emerged, a version who was more stable and rebuilt from within.

Now, I'm not saying you have to try as many modalities as I did, but I *am* saying that you have to commit yourself to going inward and dealing with the negative beliefs you hold about who you are and what you can do. Without that commitment, your success will remain elusive even when opportunities come your way. Without that inner work, you may still feel completely miserable inside even if you reach the highest levels, receive the accolades, or get married and have kids. Only by doing the inner work can you live authentically, achieve your dreams, and find true fulfillment.

My intention with writing this book is to be real, authentic, and honest. It's to write the truth of my story and what I've learned, in hopes to have a true and deep connection with women. To write what resonates, hits home, and makes you feel like "Yes, I know exactly what that feels like." One of the things I dislike the most is self-help books that sell it to you like they have all the answers. The truth is, they don't, and neither do I. Genuinely, I don't have all the answers, but I can share with all of you my experiences, pains, ups and downs, lessons, and hopes. Because being authentic, sincere, and true to everyone around me is the greatest gift and power that I have, and you have it too.

This book guides you through that process of reimagining yourself so that you can have the confidence to become the leader you're meant to be, whether that's leading a team, a class, a function, an organization, a corporate board, or a government. Remember that you have to be willing to do the work. Your transformation will take place over three phases:

Phase 1:
Believing in Yourself: Building Your Self-Worth and Confidence

Phase 2:
Building Your Team: Role Models, Mentors, and Support Groups

Phase 3:
Rising to Lead: Achieving Your Goals, Landing Your Dream Career, and Stepping into Power

Phase 1 is deep and emotional work that I will walk you through step-by-step. However, if you are someone who has spent time developing your self-worth and feel solid with yourself internally, PLEASE go ahead and skip Phase 1 and start reading this book at Phase 2.

The work you will do in Phase 1 requires introspection to define what this life means to you and what you want from it. But it's so, so worth it, and this book gets you started on that journey for yourself. If you are in your early twenties, just got fired from your dream job, or are about to make a huge life transition and feel like the world is spinning without you in it, these first few chapters are for you. The work and shared stories help build the foundation for who you want to become. We focus on uncovering your negative self-beliefs and rewriting them to build your self-worth. There are also exercises that will require you to go deep enough to find the cobwebs and boxes of misguided information embedded in your memory files.

Phase 2 focuses on building your support system. As women, we often try to do it all ourselves, myself included. Work, school, carpool, home, and so on—we try to juggle everything, only to be left exhausted and on the brink of burnout. The same goes for women wanting to build something incredible for themselves and rise into power. No one can do anything alone, especially take a seat of power in a patriarchal society. So, this phase is all about building your support system and forging those special relationships. This is about building your community of people who will believe in you, even when you don't believe in yourself.

Phase 3 is about fully stepping into your own and rising to power. This phase excites me the most. Knowing that each of us has the power within us to step into ourselves and take our rightful place on stages, on boards, in businesses, and then to lead is just . . . AH! It's about leading authentically, embracing your story, and bravely sharing yourself with the world. Because ultimately, that is what we are all here for. What is life without sharing your talents and gifts with others?

This book is for every woman who doubts her abilities and doesn't fully recognize her amazing powers. The woman who knows she is worthy of great things but can't get out of her limiting beliefs audio tapes. The woman who is ready to shine, to live unapologetically as herself but needs that one final push of encouragement and support. The woman who is seeking a community to support her on her journey to achieving success on her own terms and doing the very thing that sets her soul on fire but she is scared to do. The woman who knows what it feels like to live in a circle of insecurity and self-doubt and wants to be freed of her mind's limitations. The woman who knows what it feels like to be silenced by a man and wants to gain her courage to stand up and live life on her own terms. The woman who wants to live her greatest and most fulfilled life. The woman who wants to contribute something to society greater than what societal norm tells her is possible. The woman who wants to know she is not alone. The woman who knows the power of her authentic story and wants to embrace her voice and command rooms with respect.

As a collective, women can create so much influence and change. The bigger challenge? We must believe in ourselves enough to do it. And the truth? We are more than enough just by being us. Our voices and creativity and talents are all fully ours to have and to share with the world during this life.

Give yourself permission to embrace who you are in your entirety—your greatness, your flaws, and all the goodness you wish to bring into the world. Begin to rediscover what sparks the light within you. Give yourself permission to let go of self-judgment and live more freely. Embrace your feminine qualities and celebrate them. In fact, I want you to begin wholeheartedly seeing yourself and your life as a celebration. Right now, envision yourself in a room of friends—people who light you up—holding a glass of champagne. The lights are bright, and balloons and rainbow confetti are falling from the ceiling. Your role models, your inspirations, and your loves in life are all there to support you. Picture it clearly. This is where you're headed. Light up your heart and watch every dark room light up.

PHASE I

BELIEVING IN YOURSELF: BUILDING YOUR SELF-WORTH AND CONFIDENCE

CHAPTER 1

IMPOSTER SYNDROME IS NOT OUR FAULT

Throughout my career, I've had the opportunity to travel all over the US and participate in many large conferences as a panelist, keynote speaker, and group moderator. I've truly loved every moment at these events, not because I got to be on stage and share my story but because I always received so many lessons in return from the other women who were present. Their personal stories have impacted me deeply, to my core.

I have connected with amazing working women from all over the country from a variety of backgrounds and industries who are juggling careers, marriages, children, sports, practices, and travel plans. They range from women aspiring to be leaders to those in high positions within big corporations. Some are entrepreneurs who recently immigrated to this country and started their own businesses for the first time. Others have established careers but want to pivot and do something for themselves rather than work for a Fortune 500 company. They have all been extremely impressive and inspiring in their own ways.

At one of the conferences, I was speaking in Texas, and I met a woman named Susanna, who shared that she was excited to start her new career in real estate because it was always her dream. She was currently working in tech but was gearing up to get her real estate license and make the switch. When I innocently started asking about her next steps, however, she shared her feelings of shame.

"I'm scared of financial conversations with my clients. What if I'm not good enough and mess up the numbers for them? I don't think I could ever forgive myself. I'm also worried about my people skills. I'm not extroverted and wonder if that means I won't be a good enough agent. I'm so worried I'm going to fail that I haven't left my tech job yet." I appreciated her candid honesty, but hearing her fears broke my heart. In fact, after our conversation, I went to my car and burst into tears.

I understood Susanna all too well. Bringing my female strengths to the workplace was always a big struggle for me. As a young professional, I had the opportunity to attend meetings through our family business, which was a great experience. But nine times out of ten, whenever we would meet with venture capital firms, real estate companies, or other partners, I was the only woman in the room. I was surrounded by a sea of suits.

I continually felt out of place and like my voice didn't matter. Even more painful to admit, I felt like my voice was less valuable than those of the men in the room. I would always enter a board meeting with the same thought: *Why would any of these men care about my opinion*?

Over my years talking with women, I've learned I'm far from alone in that feeling. Take Tabitha. I first met her through a mutual friend, and we connected over our shared passion for women's empowerment. She had been a very high-level and intellectual executive for many years. She had also spent time in academia, which made her extremely knowledgeable in data and gender studies research. When we met, she had just retired to spend time with her family.

She told me about her experiences while sitting on a corporate board. Getting to sit on a corporate board is an incredible achievement, but Tabitha said it exacerbated her thoughts of not being good enough. As she was the only woman on the board, she felt like she had to constantly overcompensate to prove her worth. Because of this, she tried to talk more than anyone else.

After five years on the board, a male counterpart pulled her aside and told her that if she was more concise with her words, she would command the room and everyone's attention more effectively. She admitted that if she had just trusted her own gut and intuition about when to speak and how much, she would have been better off. Trying to prove herself to the men in the room didn't allow her to bring her best and most authentic self.

Next, let me tell you about Jennifer. As a well-known entrepreneur and executive, she grew her business into a national success story. After twenty years of being in the medical industry, she was invited to serve on a corporate board. She was able to serve for five years, and as proud as she was to be one of the few women serving, she doubted herself for the entirety of those years. She admitted to me that she was so nervous in every single meeting that she would have sores in her mouth and sweat all over her body. Even with all her business success, she couldn't get herself to believe that she belonged in that room.

These gut-wrenching stories prove that even the most successful, put-together, well-rounded, educated, talented, and well-known women battle with imposter syndrome.

Imposter syndrome is a strange and off-putting feeling. It's often been described to me as a feeling of being a fraud and not being good enough, that the whole world is going to find out you are lying and have been hiding the fact that you're indeed not good enough. For me, it's the feeling that you're a fraud at work and not capable of doing what you've been hired to do, even when you are completely qualified. Can anyone relate to this feeling?

It's a roadblock that many of us face. In fact, a KPMG study found that 75 percent of female executives across industries have experienced imposter syndrome in their careers.[1] I've sat down with literally hundreds of women across the country over the past few years and just listened. The one thing that virtually all of them have in common is that at some point, they didn't believe they could fulfill their dreams or didn't believe they deserved to fulfill them. Every woman experienced self-limiting beliefs and imposter syndrome. Clearly, it's a pattern.

And it's a pattern I personally know all too well. Since I can remember, I have been at war with myself. Even while I achieved my goals, I always felt like I was taking one step forward, only to take twenty steps back. The doubt was so loud that it often paralyzed me. Those voices said, "you're going to fail," "you won't ever make it," "you're not smart enough," and the list goes on. The voices haunted me throughout elementary school, high school, and college. No matter where I went or what I did, the voices stayed in my head. When I recognized so vividly that these statements coming from Susanna and other women like her weren't remotely true, I realized that my own inner voice wasn't true of me either. I also realized that these limiting beliefs didn't originate with us. They started outside of us.

Think back to a time when you lived freely without self-doubt. For me, it was when I was a little girl dancing and waving my hands all over the place to salsa music or A*Teens. I was authentic, real, and without a care in the world. That girl didn't start with self-doubts. She heard them from others and started to believe them. And over time, she came to see them as facts.

What "facts" do you believe about yourself that aren't facts at all? Maybe your aunt told you that girls are bad at math and finance, or maybe a man once told you that women don't have a head for business, at least not management. Somewhere along the way, someone or something made you believe inaccurate things about yourself. And there is no better time than right now to reevaluate the legitimacy of those beliefs as you read this book.

In her book *The Moment of Lift: How Empowering Women Changes the World*, Melinda French Gates writes: "In workplaces around the world, women are made to feel that we aren't good enough or smart enough. Women get paid less than men do. Women of color get paid even less. We get raises and promotions more slowly than men do. We don't get trained and mentored and sponsored for jobs as much as men do." Yet, she also says: "If you want to lift humanity, empower women. It is the most comprehensive, pervasive, high-leverage investment you can make in human beings."[2]

Remember the statistics I cited in the introduction about how female-led businesses are more successful? Any man who denies these numbers is shooting himself in the foot. Clearly, it isn't really about our ability.

A *Harvard Business Review* article calls into question the true origins of imposter syndrome, asking: Is it women who are to blame or is it the societal constructs that surround us that make us doubt ourselves? The article points out: "Even as we know it today, imposter syndrome puts the blame on individuals, without accounting for the historical and cultural contexts that are foundational to how it manifests in both women of color and white women. Imposter syndrome directs our view toward fixing women at work instead of fixing the places where women work."[3] I certainly believe that societal constructs have created the pressures that women feel in the workplace. We may be naturally quieter or more timid, but these are also qualities we have been taught.

However, we can't wait around for societal constructs to change or just hope for things to improve. The inner work we do to heal our imposter syndrome will help us make those changes in society. But first we have to believe in ourselves if we want to achieve our goals.

Progress Has Been Slow, but It's There

Our world has been created by history, people, and laws, and all of these influence the way we are programmed to see ourselves. Throughout our country's history, society has favored men over women. They have been given more political power, financial power, education, and voting rights than women. Every president elected since 1789 has been a man, and in 2024, we *still* didn't elect a woman for that job. We came close, however, which is certainly progress!

But because men have been in positions of power, they

have consistently dictated where and how the country's choices have been made. It wasn't until the early 1900s that women's rights even became a part of the dialogue. In the list that follows, you'll see different historical moments that moved women's rights ahead and made significant strides in our abilities to gain independence and power. These moments speak great volumes to how things have changed and can continue to change. Once women were allowed to work and earn a fairer (although still not equitable) wage, this was reflected in our television and media and in the way we viewed ourselves. We can continue to move in that direction.

Here's a timeline of historic moments that shaped our society with regard to women:

Legislation

1920: The 19th Amendment is ratified, guaranteeing women the right to vote.

1963: The Equal Pay Act is signed by President John F. Kennedy, protecting against wage discrimination based on gender.

1972: Title IX bans gender discrimination in education programs that are funded with federal dollars, giving women greater opportunities.

1974: The Equal Credit Opportunity Act allows women to apply for credit in their own name without a male cosigner.

Wage Gap

1960: Women make 61 cents for every dollar a man makes.

2024: Women make 82 cents for every dollar a man makes.

Labor Force Participation

Early 1900s: 20 percent of all women (5 percent of married women) are categorized as "gainful workers" by the Census Bureau.

1972: Katharine Graham becomes America's first female CEO of a Fortune 500 company.

1990: 74 percent of women participate in the labor force.[4]

Because of these amazing steps forward in government, we've been able to make strides in women's rights and empowerment. Today, the US is further ahead in gender equality than many other countries, but at the same time, we're behind some countries where women are valued more. For example, here's some of the good news and some of the bad news:

- Only 2 percent of venture capital partners are women, and only 2 percent of venture capital money goes to women-founded ventures. The amount of venture capital that goes to firms founded by African American women is 0.2 percent.[5]

- Women account for only 8.8 percent of Fortune 500 CEOs. At the same time, according to Women Business Collaborative, "Research estimates that women own 40% of all companies in America, with Black and Latina founders starting businesses in record numbers."[6]

- Latinos are seeing the least growth of any other group, however, when it comes to board representation. In 2020, they held 4.1 percent of Fortune 500 board seats.[7] Further, only 1 percent of corporate board seats are filled by Latina women.[8] Meanwhile, 62.5 million Latinos make up 19 percent of the US population. The community is large and growing. Nearly five million Latino-owned businesses in the US contribute more than $800 billion to the economy annually.[9] That's huge!

- McKinsey & Company says: "By 2030, American women are expected to control much of the $30 trillion in financial assets that baby boomers will possess—a potential wealth transfer of such magnitude that it approaches the annual GDP of the United States."[10] With the wealth scale tipping in our favor, we will have more control and buying power over time. But what good is it if we don't have equal representation in positions of power to make a difference?

I could cite countless more statistics that show both the good and the bad, and I fully acknowledge that the way women have been treated in business and society is unfair. It isn't fair that women are labeled too sensitive and emotional instead of venerable and empathetic. It isn't fair that women must take on the greatest burden of childcare. It isn't fair that women in marginalized groups have it even harder than white women. But knowing all of this gives us more power to do something about it.

It helps to recognize the true obstacles we have faced. When we see these clearly, it lets us know unequivocally that we aren't meant to buy into societal bias. These beliefs that we have taken to heart don't belong to us and have no place in our minds. The generalizations and stereotypes about women that have been ingrained in us don't define us. They have nothing to do with who we really are or who we want to be. This is why we have to work on our imposter syndrome and get ourselves ready for what's to come. If someone else doesn't value us, we have to value ourselves. The false beliefs that others hold about us are not our business—even when it's a man who scoffs at our ideas. Our beliefs are ours to create and not for others to interfere with.

At the same time, we have to acknowledge that our imposter syndrome exists. Holding back our internal dialogue and experiences is very damaging to both ourselves and other women we meet. When we hide, we model an unrealistic expectation for other women, making them think they're alone in their doubts. They think we never once doubted ourselves and that something's wrong with them because they do.

Rewriting my personal beliefs has taken some time, but once I was able to identify which beliefs came from outside of me, I could breathe again. Acknowledging that those beliefs weren't mine to carry felt like a weight lifted off my shoulders. It also helped me to see that women I admire who have accomplished so much *still* have imposter syndrome. I know unequivocally that their doubts are wrong, so what does that say about my doubts about myself? What does that say about your doubts about yourself?

EXERCISE: Imposter Syndrome Exploration

Imposter syndrome may not be our fault, but while we work on changing societal norms that hold women back, we can also work on eliminating the false beliefs that we took on from those outdated norms.

Take note of the times when you've suffered from imposter syndrome. When have you feared you weren't up to par? Have those perceptions prevented you from applying for jobs or asking for raises or advancement? Write down all the times you can remember when you felt this way, and make note of how those feelings stopped you.

CHAPTER 2

WHAT DO YOU BELIEVE ABOUT YOURSELF?

"How did you do it?" Gigi asked me as we sat outside for lunch.

"Do what?" I replied, even though I already knew where she was going.

"Get to this point. How are you so confident and self-assured?"

I paused, letting the words hang between us. The truth is that I wasn't always this way. And Gigi knew that better than anyone. As my longtime friend, she had witnessed the messy seasons, the doubts, and the years when confident was the last word anyone would use to describe me.

She leaned in, her voice softer now. "Lately I've been struggling to find my own confidence, especially with something deeper than just my work and accomplishments. How did you figure it out? And how did you learn to believe in yourself?"

I knew the answer, but I didn't want to say it. As I continued to pause, the answer was taking up the room's presence like a secret we shouldn't repeat.

"I had to do the work and really dig deep." I paused as she silently nodded her head.

"I know it's not what you want to hear, Gigi, and I'm sorry for that. But it's the truth. When I got down to the root of what was driving these beliefs, everything changed. As tough as it was in the process, I am so thankful for those tough moments when I had to face the truth of it all. Without confronting them, I wouldn't be the version of the girl you're looking at right now."

Since that moment with Gigi, so many girls and mentees of mine have come up to me and all asked the same question as Gigi: "How did you do it?" And I know the answer isn't exactly what you all want to hear, but it's the truth. I felt the same way before a turn of events forced me to hit my version of rock bottom. But don't wait to hit the floor until you do the work internally. You have the chance to make your life exactly how you want it. And even better? You have the chance to wake up and genuinely love yourself and the life you're living. But you have to get to know yourself and what makes you tick, what drives you and what's going to make you keep working toward your goals when things get tough.

When's the last time you took time for yourself? Give yourself and your dreams a chance because they deserve to be out in the world, and your life deserves to be one that you love. We have to start with what you believe about yourself and what you are telling yourself on a daily basis. I know it sucks, but to ease the pressure off you for a second, how about I go first?

If someone had asked me what I believed about myself a few years ago, I would have frozen at the thought of sharing my real thoughts. My internal beliefs included a variety of awful thoughts, like:

I'm the ultimate worst.

I hate my body. I need to lose weight.

I have no idea what I'm going to do with my career.

I feel like a loser and a failure.

As hard as it was to admit then, it was the first step to my progress. And the truth? So many of us are thinking these same thoughts. I honestly had no idea that so many women carried these thoughts within themselves, until we started sharing these pieces of ourselves online and on social media. That's one positive thing that has come out of online sharing; we are becoming more and more real and authentic with everyone around us. So here's my message to all you readers:

If I can share these thoughts with you, then you can be honest with yourself at home. You are not alone.

Nevertheless, it's an important question: What do you *believe* about yourself? Are your thoughts positive or negative? Do they light you up or make you embarrassed to say them out loud? This is a crucial part of understanding who you are and getting to the heart of your future. If you can't verbalize what you think about yourself, how can you change it?

It's hard to change our thoughts and beliefs without taking the time to think about them. Life gets busy. Calendars get booked. Schedules are tight and hard to rearrange. As we go through life, these routines become the norm, and so do our thoughts. So many of our daily facts are the same unless we make a conscious effort to think differently. Have you ever taken inventory of your thoughts? Let's pause and think about them.

Do you have thoughts that pop up on a regular basis that criticize you? Thoughts such as "Why did I just say that?" or "What was I thinking . . . I'm such an idiot"? These thoughts are your beliefs about yourself. I know how hard it is to believe that you are worthy and deserving. But even if you get an education, even if you get a great job, even if you find that person you've always been looking for, you will always feel off-kilter if you don't believe in yourself and have self-worth. You won't be able to reach your full potential because you will be in your own way, blocking yourself from being able to reach your truest goals and desires.

As I started to work on changing my negative beliefs to positive ones, I felt better. But something was missing. Although I told myself I was "strong and capable" and all the positive, empowering words, I didn't believe them deep down. Why? Because I didn't believe I was worthy. To really explain what this means, I want to call in the expert, Jamie Kern Lima. She is not only an incredible author, but she is also a wildly successful business entrepreneur. She is a highly sought-after businesswoman and role model for others. I see her being vulnerable and I think, *She's a good one*. After reading her book, I found myself reevaluating my own life and choices. Her definition of being worthy really hit home.

Jamie defines self-worth as the deep internal knowing that we're worthy of love and belonging exactly as we are.[1] Sounds great! Easy peasy, Jamie, no problem! Except it isn't and wasn't that easy for me. I hit two major roadblocks to believing I was "worthy." The main problem with living out this definition is that I didn't believe I was worthy of love and belonging exactly as I was, because my idea of being worthy was tied to my core beliefs, which created an even bigger web of problems to untangle.

With lots of reflection and time, I learned that these issues were major obstacles that stopped me from embracing myself authentically. And to get to the other side, I had to walk straight through the pain of untangling these issues head-on. I want to take time to describe my own personal untangling of these two core beliefs I had about myself, because they ended up becoming two major blocks on the road to finding my self-worth. Whatever your roadblocks are in life, know that everyone has them. And although they may take a different shape or form, the feeling is the same—feeling unlovable and unworthy of it all.

Before I could start rebuilding my confidence and self-worth, I needed to turn inward and clear out all the cobwebs. This brings us to the image you see next. This gives you an easy mental picture as to why changing your thoughts won't really change a thing. If your core beliefs are negative, you are bound to release self-limiting thoughts.

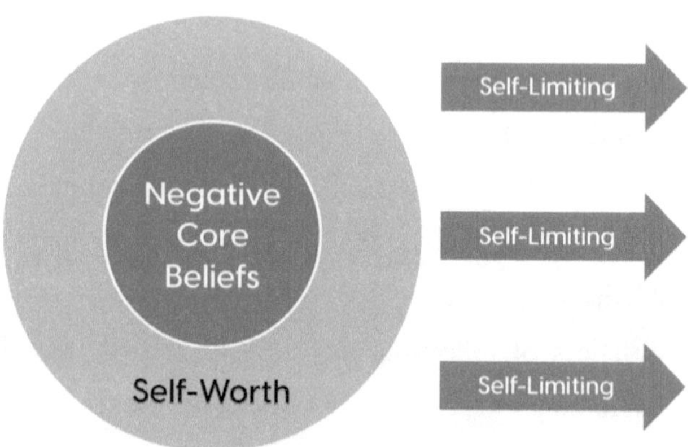

Have you ever told yourself yoga affirmations in the morning, only to forget them by the end of the day? I even tried writing a positive affirmation on a sticky note and posting it on my mirror, so I'd remember to recite it throughout the day. However, by the end of the day, I would just put on my vitamin C and serums and go to bed, completely ignoring the note. We can try to tell ourselves that our self-limiting thoughts aren't true, but if we don't alter our core beliefs, real change won't happen.

So instead of trying to change each and every negative, self-limiting thought, focus on revising your negative core beliefs. When you adjust those core beliefs, your outgoing thoughts will change as well.

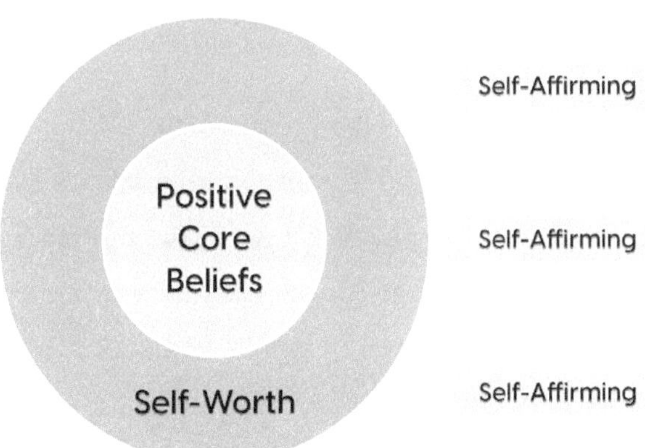

My Negative Belief #1: My Self-Worth Was Contingent Upon Career Success

Over time in my career, I started to become hyperaware of negative beliefs because I wasn't performing or creating the way I wanted to. As I discovered, my self-worth was highly attached to my output and success at work. Contributing to the bottom line through sales is one thing, but not feeling like your work is meaningful is another.

In my late twenties, I hit that wall. I could feel in my gut that something was off, and I knew I couldn't continue to live that way. The voices of self-doubt in my head were so loud that I couldn't even hear myself think. Where those voices originated—whether with coworkers, family, friends, acquaintances, or society—didn't matter. What mattered was that these fears and thoughts were holding me back from achieving my goals.

I vividly remember the day I decided I needed help. I was in an Uber going home from the airport after a work trip. In checking my emails, I found that none of the projects I had been working on got approved. In that moment, I had the sinking feeling of hitting rock bottom. I felt like I had failed myself and I didn't know anyone who could help me fix it. There was a huge disconnect between what I wanted to do and my actual job. I wanted so badly to interweave my purpose with my work, but I didn't see a clear path to do so, and I didn't know how I was going to make it possible. Not only that, but after graduating from college, I felt like a big failure because I didn't go work for one of the Big 4 Companies (PwC, Deloitte, Ernst & Young, and KPMG).

During my time at business school, I always felt like I was the ugly duckling in the room. My accounting classes never stuck with me, I failed just about every finance course I took, and everything numbers related felt like an uphill battle I could never win. I didn't land any interviews with these big-time recruiters that came to campus, and every letter stating I didn't get the job felt like a personal punch in the gut. When everyone around me was jetting off to a new big corporate job surrounded by finance bros, I was starting a completely different path in sales and marketing that at the time felt like a huge demotion.

For the rest of the car ride, I continued to go around in circles with my thoughts. I felt helpless and like I had no one to turn to. But as the car stopped, something inside of me finally clicked: If I didn't get help soon, I would be spiraling in the same thought pattern forever. I looked out the window of the car and thought, *There must be a better solution or someone who can help me through this.*

I started to mentally go through my Rolodex of women I knew in business who I could call and ask for help. But none of them had the expertise I was looking for. I remember thinking about all the women I met at conferences and replaying our conversations in my head about how they found support. And then it hit me: What if I hired a coach to help me? Many of the business leaders across industries had shared about their amazing experiences working with a coach or consultant. Women you would never think "needed help" because they were so picture perfect on stage were the first to attribute their success to their coaches and consultants. I even learned that Fortune 500 companies will budget thousands of dollars every year to women in manager and director roles for them to work with a career coach for their personal development.

So, I typed "career coach" into LinkedIn and focused on female coaches. The moment I got home, I emailed my top favorites, and after talking to them, one in particular stood out. I had a gut feeling about her and decided to trust it. That was the day I made my first investment in myself. As much as hitting rock bottom hurt, it made asking for help easier.

At times, I have felt asking for help to be tough because, by default, we are admitting we can't do something alone. But let me clear this up for all of us right here and right now: No one can do anything alone. The best things in life are created and have happened in collaboration and community with others. And those successful people sitting at the top? They all had help and support. They did not get there alone. So, if you are feeling stuck and like you don't know what your next step is or what else is even possible, take a chance on yourself, double down, and ask for help. I promise you, the response from the people around you will surprise you.

Most people want to help. They want to see others succeed and find solutions that improve their lives and the lives of others. Don't wait to hit rock bottom like I did to ask for help. Let this be your sign to invest in yourself, whatever that looks like for you. Maybe you download a meditation app on your phone to take twenty minutes of time for yourself at night to dream about your career. Or you book a one-on-one session with an incredible money coach you've been following for years whose financial advice you always wanted. Wherever you are feeling stuck, I officially grant you permission to ask for help. Book that one-on-one call with your dream financial coach or download that free meditation app to start dreaming. Investing in yourself, whether it's with your time or money, is something you will never regret.

It's funny because my success with coaching didn't happen overnight. I assumed my coach would listen to all the things I wanted to do, create my five-year plan and my ten-year plan, and then voilà, all of my problems would be solved! But boy, was I wrong in the best way. Instead, to my surprise, progress didn't start until weeks into our work together. She challenged me to go deep and answer questions like "What is your purpose in this lifetime?" and "What do you want your legacy to be?" I always thought I knew the answers to those questions, but when I had to really articulate them, I couldn't. It took weeks of deep reflection, meditation, and journaling to get me to my most profound and soul-teaching moments.

Along the journey of working with my coach, things slowly started to come together. There were ideas, inspirations, and moments of pure joy. I found myself imagining my future, where I wanted to be, and how I saw myself. Even on the treadmill, which has always been a great spot for me to visualize and read, many small answers came to me. Answers such as "Maybe I *would* be great at starting my own business" or "Maybe I *am* good enough to mentor others." My coach and I put these pieces together to create the future version of me that I wanted to be.

But the most important part of the journey was believing I deserved it. As women, we often try to please everyone else first before we get something for ourselves. How many times have you played it small because you were afraid of what others would think? We try to appease everyone and be the nice girl so that no one talks behind our back. Or we second-guess ourselves before we consider taking steps toward achieving our dreams. Then, when we do reach our goals and get what we want, we still don't believe we deserve it. I knew I had to get past those worries and out of that mindset.

Fast-forward to a couple of years later, and my coach turned out to be better than a therapist; our relationship evolved into multiple nights with friends over pizza. Working with her pulled me out of my darkest times and set me straight on a path of deep work and self-discovery. It wasn't the five-year or ten-year plan or even the to-do lists that really mattered. What mattered the most was the work I did to reevaluate my own worthiness. Not only did I learn more about myself but I was also able to clearly define from my soul what I wanted to do in this life. Better yet, I could articulate it clearly. Once I did, everything set into motion, and I was in a constant state of flow with my work.

Now my self-worth is no longer tied to my work outputs or accomplishments. My first roadblock was to release the belief that I had to achieve amazing things at work to be lovable or even love myself. Instead, it's the opposite. My love for myself always comes first, and everything else follows. It always does, and it always will.

Looking back on my time at school, I laugh because I know I was just in the completely wrong major. It wasn't clear to me then, but it is crystal clear to me now. Instead of being in the business school, I should have been learning about my true passions: writing, speaking, communications, and gender equity. I was never meant to be a "finance bro" or fit into that corporate culture on Wall Street. I was supposed to be exactly where I am now: living my purpose through my work in Corporate Social Responsibility and advocating for women.

The lesson? When things don't click at work, it's not because something is wrong with you or you aren't smart enough. It's because you're in the wrong position or industry. It's because your values, strengths, and passions aren't in direct alignment with what you are doing. It's not you; it's just the room you are in. It's one of the biggest lessons I now advocate for young women in school or starting their first job: There is no such thing as not being good enough because you fail a test or a project. They are just moments to show you what you're good at and what you should be doubling down on and spending your time and energy learning instead.

My self-worth is now tied to my connection with myself and how I impact those around me. Once I got clear about my life's purpose, I was fulfilled whenever my work aligned with that purpose. This is my greatest wish for all of you. I hope you remove the roadblocks that prevent you from believing you're worthy of everything you desire.

My Negative Belief #2: My Body Weight Had to Be "Perfect"

Besides measuring my self-worth based on my accomplishments at work, I also measured it based on my body weight. I have always been ashamed of my body, even as a young girl. All the tormented thoughts and shame I felt ultimately led me to an eating disorder at ten years old. I tried everything to be something I never was and something that was impossible to be—perfect. As a result, I hurt myself and my body, and I never once thought that something was wrong with how I treated it. I just believed I had to change it in order to be accepted by the world and the men around me.

Yet, when I look back on my childhood, a big part of my daily routine was spent around binge eating. I realize now that these moments were deeply rooted in my pain, which was an uncontrollable force. The louder the shame got, the more I ate. My daily thoughts were all consumed with food. These thoughts were the first things on my mind when I woke up and the last things before bed. *Eat this? Think again! Diving into a pool? Can't do that because you'd have to wear a bathing suit and everyone would see your body. Want to see your friends for dinner? Nope! You might overeat fries and hate yourself for a week.*

The guilt was my own form of torture. My personal favorite was "You can't eat that because you don't deserve it." I seemed to think that if I could make myself feel bad enough about overeating, I'd stop. Instead, the self-judgments just made me overeat more. Every time I binged, the words got worse. There was never a point when I was happy or at peace with my body, because I wouldn't allow myself to feel happy or be fully present unless my body was the correct weight. I continued to internally kill my spirit. I wished so badly that I could just stand up, walk over to the wall, and turn off the thoughts like a light switch.

For years, I thought I was alone in this. But in reality, so many young girls and women feel the exact same way. "According to The Center for Mental Health Services, 90 percent of those who have eating disorders are women between the ages of 12 and 25." And 59 percent of the girls surveyed reported dissatisfaction with their body shape, while 66 percent expressed the desire to lose weight.[2]

Social media continues to amplify our body insecurities. Findings from a new study have warned that social media poses a significant risk to the current and future health of today's younger generations, where three out of four children as young as twelve dislike their bodies and are embarrassed by the way they look. This increases to eight in ten young people age eighteen to twenty-one.[3]

It's a battle that so many of us have been up against, and it can feel impossible to overcome. But as I got older and started to move through the pain—the pain of feeling like I wasn't enough for others, for a relationship, for myself—I recognized that a lot of my shame and guilt didn't start within. It started from outside of me.

Societal constructs placed on women by society make us think we have to look a certain way and stay a certain bathing suit size. Knowing that these beauty standards weren't mine to live up to helped me a great deal. Through years of therapy, journaling, meditating, and support from friends, I have finally found peace with my body and mind. It hasn't been perfect or linear, but with time and practice, I have healed my past traumas and pain to arrive at a healthier place. I'm living proof that it's absolutely possible to change body image beliefs.

The truth is that you are worthy no matter what the scale says. I know the big question is: *How do you make yourself believe that you are worthy and deserving when your entire life you've told yourself otherwise?* It starts small, and it takes time to alter long-held beliefs. I had to remind myself repeatedly that my body is my sacred home, and it deserves love. Think about all the people you love. Do you really care what their body looks like? What matters to you about those people?

What We Believe About Ourselves

What would help you believe you're amazing and deserve the best? For me, it started by realizing that it was unfair to put society's values on myself. I realized that my self-worth had to come from within and be unwavering regardless of what happened in my external world.

I didn't base the self-worth of others on their accomplishments or their bodies. So why did I do that to myself? I realized I couldn't allow anyone to shake or change my sense of self-worth. If I relied on others to make me believe I was worthy, I would also be vulnerable to their harsh words. And if I believed those harsh words from others, then I would lose my sense of purpose. I recognized that, as women, we must listen to our intuition and gut feelings. They are the most powerful resources for staying in touch with our true purpose and true value. Sure, there are times when our inner critic may be loud, but we can learn to stay anchored in our strengths, knowing that we have value that no one else can take away.

Today, if someone asked me what I believe about myself, my answer would be drastically different than in the past. I would say, "I believe I can do great things in this life. I believe I'm an amazing author and guide for young women, and I exude positivity and love to the people around me." To my younger self, that's quite a revelation. And a big change. The best part is that writing it here for you to read feels natural and wonderful because I truly believe those words.

So, let's work toward getting you to believe it! Journaling is one of the most amazing tools I have learned to use through my healing and self-discovery process. Tara Schuster, one of my favorite authors, used journaling as a way to heal her past traumas and find her new self. I started doing Julia Cameron's "Morning Pages," as she suggests in her book *The Artist's Way*. Morning Pages are a journal exercise where you freewrite up to five pages in order to develop self-intuition and a clear understanding of yourself. Journaling allowed me to go after my creative endeavors without self-doubt or ego stopping me from trying. It is our very right to create in this world as humans, and who are our self-doubt and inner critic to stop us from trying?

Journaling allows you to write without judgment, without restriction, without an agenda. It's a way to let your subconscious thought get out from your mind and onto the page. When I first started this activity, I sometimes didn't know what to write. I would stare off blankly at the wall and into space, thinking about all the things I had to do that day. But the moment I allowed my pen to just start writing whatever came from my gut without judgment was when the pen started flying. Tapping into your deep subconscious and free-flowing thoughts is where all your magic lies.

I learned that I could release a lot of my internal thoughts onto the pages. Knowing that no one else would read the words and that they belonged wholly to me, I was gifted with privacy of mind and space. It allowed my judgmental thoughts to quiet down. Whenever something was bothering me or I felt off, I could write for twenty minutes and get to the bottom of it. Out came all my insecurities and worries. Then, after weeks of journaling, I began to uncover my underlying limiting beliefs.

Give it a try! Start writing in your journal or Notes app every morning with the intention of filling three pages with whatever you're thinking.

Besides that, do the exercises that follow. Then be patient with yourself. As I said, this takes time and practice. It's a process, not something that happens overnight. But I promise you that if you put in the effort, you can change your limiting beliefs and begin to believe in yourself and your dreams fully.

EXERCISE: What Are Your Negative Beliefs About Yourself?

Do you believe you are deeply worthy of all good things? The answer should be ABSOLUTELY YES! But as was true for me for a long time, you may not believe it. Let's take a moment to dig deep and break down some of the barriers that could be holding you back.

- What are some of the beliefs you currently hold about yourself? The point of putting them on paper is to release them from inside of you and get them out of you and onto the paper. Once you see them on paper, you start to realize that they aren't true.

    - ______________________________
    - ______________________________
    - ______________________________
    - ______________________________

- Now, write a mini letter to yourself to address and release these old beliefs. Be specific and say exactly what you feel and how you're releasing them for good. When you're finished, rip the letter up and throw it away. Throwing it away signifies that you are no longer bound to these beliefs and are starting fresh. Here is an example of a short letter I wrote:

I no longer believe these things are true. I'm letting go of these words that had power over me, because I can choose what I want to believe. And I choose not to believe anyone else's opinion but my own. These words no longer have power over me.

- Now that you have intentionally walked yourself through mentally removing those thoughts and beliefs, you can work on creating and implementing new ones.

This is about turning inward and rebuilding the love you once had for yourself, because you are loved and worthy of all good things.

It's time to write your new *core beliefs*. Think BIG! Don't hold back! What are the most amazing, beautiful, wondrous, exciting things you want to believe?

- ____________________
- ____________________
- ____________________
- ____________________

CHAPTER 3

CREATING YOUR DREAM SELF: THE NEW YOU

I was traveling with Sophia Mason, a dear friend of mine who is one of the most brilliant and resourceful women I know. She works for a Fortune 500 company, and her career has always been top of mind and on the up and up. She falls into the category of "aspirational" friends, as she does things that scare or intimidate most people and does them with full confidence and ease.

We were in the airport, sitting in the terminal, waiting to catch our flight. We sipped our double shot lattes and talked about our careers, one of our favorite things to do. I started telling her about my new projects and what I was working on. Nodding her head, she asked to hear all about it. I took out my notebook and pen and started rattling off a few bullet points. As I started reading them out loud, I caught myself forgetting a few things. I hadn't had the time to write down a few thoughts that I had been working on, and Sophia silently but visibly gasped.

"Do you always write everything in your notebook?"

"Yes! I mean, not everything," I embarrassingly admitted, "but for the most part. Why? Where else would I put it?" Sophia quickly whipped out her phone and showed me something that was about to change my entire writing and creativity process.

"I use my Notes app and put every little thing in here. It has turned into my very own library of work."

I paused and glanced at her notes. Things as silly as "funniest jokes" to "best places to eat in LA" to "work to-do list" were all on there. I couldn't believe she had so much information in this app, and all easily searchable. Personally, the only thing I had ever kept on there were old photos and passwords to TV logins I could never find. But when it came to my work and looking something up, I had to remember where in my journals I had written it down. There was something traditional but also calming about it. But as I scrolled through her notes, I saw dozens of lists, notes, ideas, and talks listed right there on her phone. Intrigued, I decided I would take her advice.

I had purchased *The Aladdin Factor: How to Ask for What You Want—and Get It* to read on the flight home. The authors, Jack Canfield and Mark Victor Hansen, believe that the most important thing we can do is write down what we want in order for it to come true. More specifically, they urge readers to write down one hundred wishes.[1] Considering I had a few hours to kill on that flight, I decided to take them up on it.

I opened my Notes app on my phone and typed a list of one to fifty. The first fifty wishes came to me easily, but after that, I *really* had to think. Canfield and Hansen were right; it's hard to come up with a hundred things because most people don't know what they want or dream for themselves![2] But what better place to start contemplating life than on a long flight where you have designated alone time to think without distractions or literally anywhere else to be?

Sitting there trying to complete this task forced me to daydream without any limitations—from small wishes, such as finding a personal stylist one day, to big wishes, such as traveling to watch the fireworks over the Sydney harbor. I even allowed myself to stretch the limitations of what I thought was reality versus imaginary by asking for a limitless supply of ice cream and purses. (A girl can dream.)

As I went through my list, I noticed a pattern. It was easy for me to write down the actual objects and dreams I wanted, but it was difficult for me to write down *who* I wanted to become and what that life looked like exactly. When I tried, I was stuck—the words stopped coming, and the ideas came to a halt. Who was it that I really wanted to be, and what was it that I wanted to share? And that got me thinking. How many of us can't vocalize or put into words who we want to become or how awesome we already are? How many of us have a difficult time telling others about ourselves? Why can't we describe ourselves as we describe our best friends? Why was it so hard for me to write down personal things about myself?

We go through life on autopilot, thinking the same thoughts, making the same decisions, and going through the motions. Going through the motions might not be the best, but we do it anyway because that is often the easy option. And as women, we have trained ourselves to play it small, to not dare talk about ourselves or our achievements because we would seem "vain and self-absorbed" to the outside world. That talking about ourselves, our likes and dislikes, would make us seem "self-obsessed." That sharing who we are could have the potential to get us into trouble. So instead, we hide ourselves. We hide our thoughts, our perspectives, the personal things about ourselves. We are afraid to express our opinions, our personalities, our favorite things, and our least favorites.

But the truth is that if you don't know what you want, how can you clearly and articulately ask for it? And if you don't know *who* you are, how can you authentically share yourself with the world? And if you can't share yourself with the world, how can others learn from your example or reach for their dreams because they saw you achieve the same goals?

Being able to visualize other women in positions of power is so important because doing so allows us to see ourselves in jobs, positions, and ideals that we never had for ourselves. It also helps us push ourselves more than what we thought we were capable of. My role models are the ones that make me think, *I didn't even know that was possible for me.* When we see someone else pushing the boundaries of what we thought was possible, we allow for new possibilities and ideas to enter our world. We start to see opportunities differently because we start to imagine ourselves in them. We start to remove memories of what we thought was always destined for us and grant ourselves permission to dream in Technicolor.

Now, describe yourself to me in the same number of details you would describe your role model or those women you look up to. Can you as excitedly explain to me why *you* are a great example for other women? Can you tell me about yourself in detail and with 100 percent positive energy? I certainly couldn't.

Let's take this even further. Can you tell me your likes, dislikes, favorite shows, travel bucket list, strengths, weaknesses? Can you tell me what your ideal weekend looks like? What about where your favorite coffee shop is? What drives you to keep going? What clothes make you feel most confident? What is your favorite flower? What do you LOVE the most about life? What do you dislike the most about life? What are the top foods you'll never eat? Who do you call in case of emergency? Where would you like to go in the next year? What small things make you smile?

The point is, I honestly found it challenging to write

down a hundred wishes I wanted in this life because most of us don't ever spend the time to think of them. It ended up taking me hours to write down even half of the list, and I still had fifty more to go. Ever since that flight, I've kept the "100 Wishes" list on my phone, and over the years, I've gone back to it and crossed off the things that came true. And you'd be surprised how many of them happened. Things I thought would take years or never happen came true within the year. And it's moments like those that make us realize how powerful these moments of dreaming up our future selves truly are.

Now, I would be remiss if I didn't include a little bit of the woo-woo magic and manifesting in this chapter. It is all part of the process of knowing who you want to become. I fully recognize that not everyone is down with the idea that you can dream up a wish and have it magically come true; point taken from my analytical girlies. BUT there is something useful in writing down what you want and working diligently to make it come true. And 80 percent of the battle is writing it down. Because once you have it down on paper, it's up to you to think about it, bring it up to your list of things to do, and go make it happen!

Now, for my woo-woo girlies, hear me out. When you are thinking and daydreaming about your future, there is an element of your imagination that just takes over. It is the part that allows you to imagine things that don't exist in your daily reality. THAT is the energy I want you to be in when you start to think about who you want to become and what you really want to achieve.

The only person who knows what you want and what will make you happy is *you*. And if you take other people's advice without consulting your own gut and intuition first, you will not only regret it and kick yourself later but you will also wonder why you ever listened to that person in the first place. Ironically, it happens more often than we want to admit. Sometimes we want to people please, and sometimes family, friends, and coworkers put pressure on us to take their advice or live the way they want us to live. But at the end of the day, the only person who knows what will make you happy is you. And the only person who knows the type of career you want, the type of business you want to create, the type of love you want to find is YOU.

When I look back at my life, I realize that almost all the things that have happened were because of manifesting. Sometimes this becomes so integral within our lives that we forget we are "manifesting" our own realities, but I promise you that it's real and part of our lives. At the time, I may not have known I was doing it, but visualizing and working toward something made things happen. Getting accepted into an Australian study abroad program, moving to my dream city, speaking on stages, and even writing books—all those dreams came true. The thoughts that we have and the words that we speak ultimately become reality in our lives. So, whether you are on the more woo-woo or less woo-woo side of things, just know that doing this work is going to make dreams and goals go in your favor.

A study conducted by Dr. Gail Matthews at Dominican University of California found that participants who wrote down their goals, made action commitments, and sent weekly progress reports to a supportive friend achieved a 76 percent success rate—a significantly higher outcome compared to groups who only thought about, wrote, or shared their goals without ongoing updates.[3] Suffice it to say that ever since that flight home with Sophia, I have kept my Notes app close to me for this reason exactly.

Anything and everything that I envision for myself gets written down immediately. Whether it's something as simple as an outfit inspiration that I want to wear or a big goal I want to achieve for myself, it all gets written down. It has become one of my biggest life hacks (no gatekeeping here) that sounds so simple but has drastically changed the way I think and work. Even for my everyday job, so many of the things I write down on my way to work or walking on the treadmill get pulled up and shared with my team or with young women I am mentoring. I use it as a tool across the board to quickly share and document my thoughts, and I highly recommend giving it a shot if you haven't already. Otherwise, I have come to find that my thoughts—and boy, do we have thousands of those a day—get lost and forgotten.

Hopefully as I told my story, you were starting to think about a few of your own wishes. I want you to keep thinking about and imagining them. Give yourself a moment to dream without limitations. The wildest and biggest dreams you can imagine for yourself. The ones you're scared to say out loud in fear of someone hearing you.

Before you begin, though, take a few moments to pour yourself your favorite drink and pull out your favorite notebook and pens or open your Notes app. Pretend that you are the girl getting interviewed in *Cosmopolitan* magazine where they write down their Q&A answers on a page and sign it with their cute signature. I believe today it is called the "Cosmo Quiz." (But this reference is for my fellow '90s babies who know exactly what I'm talking about and the excitement you got flipping to that page to find out that person's favorite things.) Well, my friend, you are now the person being interviewed.

Now imagine that the interviewer asks you to describe your ideal weekend. This weekend is just for you; no one else is making decisions on what you do. You have FULL control over the itinerary. So . . . what does your ideal weekend look like? Are you spending the day going to museums? Are you cooking new recipes? What food are you eating? Are you having fun with friends or spending time with family? What are you wearing? What music are you listening to? What wine are you drinking? How many hours are you spending at each activity?

Now that you know what you'd like to do during an ideal weekend, think about your ideal career, your ideal life, your ideal legacy. What are the things you want for yourself? Who is the person you want to become? What is it you want to achieve? If you picked up this book, it is most likely because you are a woman who wants to rise to power either in your career or your personal life. Can you envision a woman in her career who you admire and want to emulate? Can you picture her in your head? What does she do, what does she wear to work, and what inspires you the most about this individual?

EXERCISE: Your Wishes

It doesn't matter if you use this page, a journal, a notebook, or a Notes app, just write. Let your wishes and dreams come directly from within *you*! These wishes are your future. Remember, you are worthy and deserving of every single one of them. And don't worry, I won't ask you to write one hundred wishes, just a few to get you started.

- Imagine yourself five years from now. What are three adjectives that you would use to describe your future self?
    - ______________________________
    - ______________________________
    - ______________________________

- Imagine you had a magic genie. Write one wish for your health, one for your relationships, and one for your career.
  - ____
    ____
  - ____
    ____
  - ____
    ____

- What is one dream you've had since childhood that still excites you today?
  - ____
    ____

- Imagine someone introducing you for an award on stage. What do they say about you?
  - ____
  - ____
  - ____

continued

- If your future self wrote you a thank-you letter, what would she thank you for?
    - ____________________
    - ____________________
    - ____________________

CHAPTER 4

BUILDING THE CONFIDENCE WE ALL DESERVE

Confidence is both simple and complex. We've all heard the familiar phrase "You can do anything if you set your mind to it." But what people rarely talk about are the fear, doubt, and anxiety that often stand in the way of actually starting.

So, I'm breaking confidence down into steps—real, actionable ones. Because confidence isn't about perfection; it's about building small touchpoints you can look back on to remind yourself that you are capable, knowledgeable, and valuable. Each step becomes proof that you can do hard things. And that proof becomes your foundation to building your confidence, because these touchpoints are facts about yourself, ones that are undeniable and will allow you to finally give yourself permission to have confidence. So, are you ready to start proving it to yourself?

Step 1: Defining Your Strengths

Some of my first moments being on stage took place within my home growing up. Every Christmas Eve, I would wait in anticipation for my cousins to arrive at our house. As the girls walked through the door, I would immediately grab their hands and run to our faux practice dance studio in the garage.

For the next two hours, we would have our very own dance practice. The songs of the Spice Girls and S Club 7 and Play were our anthems, and we would create a mashup dance recital to all our favorites from each album. We would spend hours practicing, tucked away from all the aunts and uncles. As they would come to the door, we would scream, "We're not ready yet, don't look!" It was clearly the performance of the year.

Once dinner was cleared and dessert was served, it was our time to shine. We would giddily take our boom box, click the CD into place, plug it into the wall, and prepare to blast it on high volume. As our favorite songs came on, we would go running in circles around the big dinner tables in our garage. I didn't realize it then, but it was the start of my fearlessness of performing. I would run around without *verguenza*, which in English means shame. I didn't let anything hold me back from teaching the choreography and practicing the dances over and over until we were ready to collapse and wait for Santa Claus to arrive.

My true personal sparkle came alive through music, food, and storytelling. As a child, I was in constant motion, spinning around in circles or ensuring everyone was on beat while hitting every move to the music of Cuban legends like Celia Cruz and Willy Chirino. When people would ask where I learned how to dance, my mom and I would look at each other, puzzled, and answer, "It's in our blood."

At that young age, I was the same "Cuban" kind of brave and confident as my grandparents, and I never held back. I was charismatic and "demonstrated great leadership skills," as Sheryl Sandberg has recommended that we describe ourselves.[1] I found great joy in dancing and leading others. It was how I expressed myself. From hip hop to ballet, I took every class. I ran there after school and immediately jumped right into the routines. I was full of laughter and excitement for the opportunity to shine on stage (as a Leo does).

That feeling of excitement continued throughout my life, especially when I had a microphone in my hand. Fast-forward to 2021, and I found myself on stage again. This was the first professional speaking engagement I would participate in, and I was speaking about my role within our organization and what we did to make an impact as a business. I knew it was a great opportunity to share with the audience our company's values, capabilities, and vision for the future. I didn't know whether I had the experience or was ready to do so. But I came to the realization that by staying quiet and not sharing my story, I was holding back the very element that others could resonate with and be inspired by, the very component that could exemplify to other women how to find their voice and not shy away from being on stage and sharing their story.

The day of the conference came, and I was uncertain and a bit nervous, but surprisingly, a small part of me knew I could do it. And that small bit of unwavering faith in myself is what allowed me to get the truest and greatest message out. Before getting on stage, in true Gabrielle Bernstein fashion, I asked the universe to "allow for me to do what is best for the highest good of all"[2] and guide me to deliver my message that needed to be heard that day. I had practiced, I felt prepared, and now it was time. I got on stage, and when I was asked what advice I would give to other female Latinas in the room and how my experiences had shaped my career, I allowed my genuine and real answers to come out. I held nothing back and spoke straight from the heart.

Afterward, I was so proud to have represented our company, and deep down, I knew I had the ability to do something as crazy as speak in front of eight hundred people and not mess up. That was one moment I am most proud of. I'll never forget walking off the stage the first time and seeing a crowd of women waiting to speak to me. That moment validated something about myself that I always knew in my gut, ever since I was little. Getting on stages and performing didn't scare me; instead, it was something I not only enjoyed but something I was also good at! It was a strength. Public speaking was a gift I had because fear never held me back.

People have asked me if I get nervous, but truthfully, I think the excitement overrides being nervous. The only way I can describe it is as a feeling of fearlessness that I can't explain or justify, but it somehow comes out whenever I am on stage. I don't sit there and doubt myself or get nervous; I just get up there and start. I channel the same little girl who would perform for her family during Christmas, walk on stage, and be myself.

The more I spoke at conferences, the more women I connected with, and the more my confidence grew. I felt stronger every time I shared our message, and I received feedback from women feeling the same exact way. Every time I got off stage, a light bulb would go off. Connecting with women on a deeper level is what I loved to do. Knowing they had probably felt the same in the workplace built this special bond between us. As we continue to evolve, we surprise ourselves. We do things we were always afraid of or thought we weren't good enough for.

Over my career, I have come to learn from reflection and time that my strengths are public speaking, writing, leading teams, empathizing, planning, creativity, and working with others. I have also learned that I am happiest when I am in service of others and using my strengths. I have always been able to connect to women, knowing the challenges and the thoughts and doubts many of us have about ourselves. I am naturally emotional and intuitive and can pick up on the way others are feeling. I have always been in tune with how someone else is feeling in the moment and how my words can impact that person.

Recognizing my strengths and using them every day is what fueled my confidence. The more I spoke, the better I got, and the more confidence and self-assurance I had in my abilities. It really was such a light bulb moment. Once I could articulate what my strengths were, I made a point to use them every day. And I started to delegate my weaknesses instead of spending hours of painful time and energy trying to accomplish something I was terrible at. What I've learned is that using our strengths can catapult us into success if we dedicate the time to improving as a daily practice.

DESIGNING YOU, BY YOU, FOR YOU

What are your strengths?

- ______________________________
- ______________________________
- ______________________________

What topics and interests light you up inside?

- ______________________________
- ______________________________
- ______________________________

If you are having trouble naming a few interests, circle the ones that resonate the most. The list of opportunities is ENORMOUS, so this is just a small list to get you going on sparking your joy:

- Analytics: Data interpretation, financial planning, measuring objectives through data
- Event Planning: Coordinating people, places, and all things
- Performing: Speaking, dancing, singing, acting, comedy
- Organizing and Managing Projects: Leading a team by keeping projects organized
- Creative: Artist, writer, designer, big thinker, brainstormer
- Music: Writing music, playing music, performing
- Business: Entrepreneur, CEO, creator
- Medicine: Hospitals, health care, helping patients
- Government: Mayor, governor, public office
- STEM: All things science, tech, engineering, and math

Step 2: Practicing

What really makes someone confident? I discovered the answer to that question through my own trial-and-error experience at one of my first jobs in sales. I was packaging and wrapping samples and then selling product to food suppliers.

When I started, I had this idea that being in sales meant I had to nail the pitch and close the deal on the first meeting. But when I picked up the phone to do my first cold call, I froze. How in the world was I supposed to talk to a stranger on the phone about a product? In that moment I felt like running away and never coming back.

But as my boss came over to my desk and asked how things were going, the pit in my stomach grew. I was horrified to tell her the truth but knew I needed to. With one last hurrah, I decided to pick up the phone and try again, but this time with a script. When they answered, I read the script verbatim, paused and took a deep breath, and then waited for them to respond. They kindly said they already had a provider but wished me luck on the sales journey. After I hung up, I thought, *Well, that wasn't so bad.* So I dialed another number and tried again. That day, I made over two hundred calls, and of the two hundred calls, ten gave me a maybe, and two said yes. I was ecstatic!

But the bigger lesson I learned was that I got better at the pitch every time I called. Not only that, but I started to refine and improve my ability to talk to people. Giving the pitch didn't seem so scary after the thirtieth one, and I got comfortable making calls. Looking back, I still can't believe how scared I was to pick up the phone. But haven't we all had that moment—fear of doing something for the first time, only to look back and realize it wasn't as bad as we thought?

For me, confidence came from and always grew with getting good at something. The more you do something, the better you get at it, the more confident you feel, and the smaller that inner critic gets. Silence the doubt by believing in yourself and knowing your worth. You must love all of yourself—your abilities, your strengths, your inner beauty, your capabilities, your flaws. You must trust your intuition, recognize what brings you joy, and realize what you're naturally inclined to do. Confidence comes from feeling great about what you are doing and knowing deep down that you are not only good at something but are also worthy of everything you are receiving and accomplishing. Start using your strengths every day.

A study done to learn about building creative cultures reports that the process of designing and building, testing, failing, and retesting will also help people begin to realize that "failure" is okay and is a necessary step on the path to success.[3] It won't be instant or overnight, but one day you will realize that those voices aren't quite as loud as they used to be. Then as the days and weeks go by, you will wake up knowing your worth and believing in your abilities, and the opinions of others and gaining their approval will matter less and less to you. My new belief system allowed me to stay secure in my everyday activities, and beyond that, my new belief system helped my self-confidence grow little by little. Every day instead of telling myself I couldn't do it, I would think, *Oh, wait a second; that's not true.*

One of the things I love doing to prepare for speaking on stages is practicing on the treadmill. As I am walking, I say out loud how I would address the room. At first, it's always rough, with so many moments where I'll start talking and then laugh at myself for saying something totally off script. But it's a part of the process, and I have so much fun with it. By the end of my walk, I'll have practiced a few times how I want to say my presentation, I'll note what came out right and what didn't, and sometimes I'll get inspiration or think of new ideas to add. It also helps me with my confidence. The more I practice out loud, the more confident in myself I get. And there is something about walking—trust me, it sounds like a lot to multitask, but focusing on walking and not falling off the treadmill helps my mind to just say out loud what I want to say without judgment, and those are the things that I end up saying on stage.

Step 3: Putting Your Inner Critic to Sleep

Elementary school was my very own form of torture. The boys at school were relentless in their pursuit to taunt and make fun of the girls in my class. They would ask what size dress we all wore and compare among the class. Height, weight, and size were all topics of discussion. And forget it if you were wearing the wrong brand of sneaker; the cool kids wouldn't even bother looking your way.

I no longer walked into the classrooms as this confident, bubbly girl. I started to compare and equate my physical looks to my worth in the world. I started to believe the things others would tell me: that I wasn't pretty enough, that I wasn't good enough, that I wasn't smart enough. That girls were bad at math, and that boys were smarter. That boys only liked pretty girls. That girls were weak and could never compete with boys. That boys' sports were better than girls' sports. All the things that were told to us through school, classmates, the media, movies, television, the list goes on. Once social media came into the picture when I was in high school, the competition just got worse.

I wish I had known then what I could do and what was in store for me in the future. I wish someone had told me, so I wouldn't have wasted my entire youth and my twenties torturing myself with horrible thoughts of self-hate, failure, and shame. We all have insecurities and struggles. We all have negative thoughts about ourselves. We all are scared to share with each other these insecurities, even though having these insecurities unites us all. We all have human minds that sometimes cause us to question ourselves. Everyone at some point will have thoughts of not being able to accomplish something. As little girls, we are told how we look is how confident we should be, and less emphasis is put on our accolades and accomplishments. And I took that belief with me everywhere. I wish someone would have shared with me that time is better spent loving and appreciating yourself, knowing your value, and believing you are remarkable.

When I work with girls one-on-one as their mentor through my mentorship program, my greatest desire is for them to believe in themselves the way I believe in them. I know deep down that they are all capable of being incredible. But I can sense the fear, the self-doubt, the thoughts of "I'm not good enough" and "I don't know what I am doing. How will I get there?"

We all have these thoughts and feelings. It's easy to think, *Am I the only one feeling this way?* In fact, a report from YPulse research group and the authors of *The Confidence Code for Girls* found that today's girls often experience low levels of confidence.

- Around three in four teen girls worry about failing.
- Between ages eight and fourteen, girls' confidence levels drop by 30 percent.
- Between their tween and teen years, girls' confidence that other people like them falls from 71 percent to 38 percent—a 46 percent drop.
- Between ages twelve and thirteen, the percentage of girls who say they're not allowed to fail increases by 150 percent.[4]

The truth is many of us don't believe in ourselves—not because we lack ability or talent, but because someone told us or made us feel as if we weren't good enough. No matter your gender or age or religion, everyone has this self-doubt inside at some point during their day or week or year or life. If we want to silence that voice of self-doubt, we need to focus internally: **It's an inside job**.

I remember watching Michelle Obama's interview with Oprah Winfrey, and a lot of girls were asking her tons of questions. The one that struck me was, how do you deal with your fearful mind? Michelle replied that she knits. Knitting helps to calm her mind and silence her worries. I find that so interesting, and I wanted Michelle to continue and give us more detail! I wanted to know how she did it and what her secrets were and how she walked into boardrooms and onto stages without fear. But that was her secret: knitting. Which, to be honest, was the last thing I thought was going to come out of her mouth on stage. But if it works for her, it just goes to show that everyone can have something different that works for them. Again, take what works for you and make it your own because everyone is different.

It's funny because the amount of self-doubt that came rushing in while writing this book shocked me. Every time I would write another page, the self-critic in me would think, *Who even cares? Who is even going to read this?* So many of us can relate to creating something and being scared to share it with the world, but we must remind ourselves that every person has their own special shine to them. That it doesn't matter how many authors have come before us or how many great inspirational speakers there have been, because there's no one like you. No one else has your energy, your thoughts, your uniqueness, or your spin on things. You could be explaining something to someone, and it could sound so different from the way someone else tells the story or describes something. But all those elements are what come together to make you and your story stand out, to make you different from the rest. And that's why each of our voices is so valuable today.

Even when women do make it to the top, the problem still exists. We still have negative thoughts and feelings of self-doubt. Is it something we continue to carry throughout our lives? We have to remind ourselves daily that we belong there, that we deserve to sit in those seats, that our voices have value. I don't think the self-doubt ever fully goes away. When those negative thoughts come to mind, the best thing we can do is prove ourselves wrong. As we are going after our dream job, as we are about to step on stage, as we are about to submit our final thesis, just for a moment, silence those thoughts of self-doubt and do it. Finish the job interview, finish your speech, and submit the thesis, despite the inner doubt. Prove yourself wrong.

Why do I so strongly believe that women must find their confidence and self-worth? Because if we don't value ourselves and believe in ourselves, then we will never get from point A to point B, let alone believe we deserve to have the same powerful position that a man has. Confidence is the jet fuel that will push you into positions of power you didn't believe you could ever achieve. I would describe it as the moment of walking into a room and owning it. It's the moment when you, at your core, believe that you are not only the best person for the job but also the most unique and exceptional person for the job. It's a feeling within you that becomes undeniable. The core, steadfast, deep knowing that you, regardless of your ethnicity, race, gender, religion, or socioeconomic status, belong and deserve it. Confidence doesn't come from what you look like externally or what you do; it comes from within.

When you put all these steps together—building your confidence and what confidence means to you—the best way I can describe it is simply in a mini equation:

Your Strengths + Practice – Self-Doubt = Confidence

I have found this equation to be true in my life, and it has helped me see that confidence doesn't come naturally. When you're feeling stuck, come back to this equation and get yourself back in alignment with your strengths. Give it time and practice, and your confidence should come through over time. Again, there is no perfect equation or solution, but I wanted to share what has worked in my life in hopes you can apply it however you find it most useful. Allow this to meet you exactly where you are.

PHASE II

BUILDING YOUR TEAM: ROLE MODELS, MENTORS, AND SUPPORT GROUPS

CHAPTER 5

ADVOCATING FOR OURSELVES AS WOMEN

When thinking about the male mentors that have come into my life, there is one I want to share with you all. At one of my speaking engagements, I was connected to an organization that does incredible work advocating for, educating, and creating opportunities for supporting Hispanics in corporate America. I was lucky enough to meet the president of the organization, Cid Wilson, who, quite frankly, has set the bar so incredibly high for male leaders. In my eyes, he is incredible not because of his career achievements, but for how he puts others' needs before his own, specifically the needs of women.

I got to know Cid personally at a dinner. The board members of their organization were in town for a meeting and wanted to connect over shared initiatives. After I sat down, he told me his story. Cid is a Dominican American and started his career in corporate America. He attributed the reason for his success in climbing the corporate ladder to a mentor he had at an early age. This mentor inspired and pushed Cid to believe in himself, and he also spoke on Cid's behalf and advocated for his promotions in the boardroom. Without this mentor, Cid wouldn't be where he is today. Now Cid has over thirty years of corporate finance and Wall Street equity research experience. He works closely with CEOs and board directors to increase the representation of Hispanics at all levels in corporate America.

I knew he was an extremely impressive man, but what really blew me away was when he took the stage at a conference a few months later. I can truthfully say that up until that point in my career, I had never seen a man inspire and vouch for women as well as Cid did that day. He spoke to a crowd of over three hundred women in corporate America and shared his hopes for all of them. His goal, his deepest hope for all the women in the room, was to inspire them and educate them. He took the time to individually speak to every woman in the room, providing his honest support and step-by-step guidance on how to get tapped on the shoulder to serve on a corporate board.

Currently, only 1 percent of board seats in America are represented by Hispanic women. Yes, you read that correctly. Coming from a Hispanic background, I witnessed firsthand extended family, family friends, and others in the community raising their children with the mentality that women should serve men, that women with aspirations were silly. And many Hispanics in America still believe that today. But hearing from Cid that it's possible shook the room, and his encouragement will continue to have a ripple effect. It expanded everyone's beliefs about herself and what they could achieve. He urged each woman in the room to go for it, to put herself out there, to get board experience.

He was transparent and shared the key insights on how we could get there, all the secrets and details of how men are doing it today. He made me feel as if it were possible. That it wasn't out of reach to dream about sitting on a board one day. The biggest thing he shared was to get experience. Start now and sit on as many boards as you can, and it can be any type of board: a nonprofit, a local group, a business event. What matters most is that you are getting leadership experience outside of your everyday role. Because the more board experience you have, the better chances you have of getting tapped on the shoulder to serve for something much bigger.

I am still in shock and awe of how supportive he was, because deep down, he truly cares and wants women to achieve positions of power, to represent our people, and to ensure that Latinas are being heard. I was so deeply moved by his presentation. It was genuine and humble. His message was loud and clear: Corporate America needs fair representation and more women in power.

I share this story about Cid because unfortunately not all men are equally supportive. Today, there are men who are firmly against feminism. There are men who don't want to support our successes, whether out of fear, lack of inner confidence, or insecurities. And there are plenty of men online who will put women down. My hope is that more men like Cid become advocates. We need men who are in full support of women taking positions of power to advocate for us and teach us, not hide behind their own egos and fears that women will take their positions or become more successful than they are. Because this isn't about that. We won't get anywhere in a world where men rule and women are at home. We need both sitting present at the table in parity for a successful and healthy society.

I am thankful every day to have been there that day to hear Cid speak and to experience what it feels like to be guided and believed in the way he believed in all of us. Since then, I have been on the lookout for more men like Cid. I believe they exist because Cid is out there. He is the ultimate cheerleader for women. We just need more of them. We need more of them advocating for us, teaching us, and wanting us to succeed. We need more of them to see us as a value add to the bottom line and overall success of a company.

I am also thankful for this experience because I got to see Cid advocating for Latina women, encouraging us, teaching us, and helping Latinas to get into positions of power. And just as he is doing for us, we need to do for ourselves because once we get inside those doors, it's up to us to speak up and continue to advocate. Not only for ourselves but also for the women who will come behind us and for those who look up to us for inspiration. Unfortunately, not everyone is raised believing these things. Attending this conference had me thinking about my own upbringing and the childhood of many Latinas around me. There is a reason that Latinas lack representation across all boards, and I want to share with you all a bit deeper as to why.

I come from a family entirely of Cubans. Both of my parents are Cuban, and my grandparents on both sides fled the country in the 1960s for the chance at a better life. They ended up in Los Angeles, where my parents ultimately met. Coming from a communist country, my grandparents risked a lot. They couldn't speak English, they had no family in the US, and they bravely left all of their loved ones behind.

My mom was born in Bejucal, a small rural town on the west side of the island. Her family was accustomed to a life that wasn't truly their own. Speaking out against the government was illegal. If they did, they could be thrown in jail. When Fidel Castro took over in Cuba, he addressed the country and announced that if anyone didn't agree with his reign, they had a small window of time to flee. That's when my mom and her parents decided to leave. When I asked my grandma Emilia how she gained the courage to leave her country, she said she felt they didn't have any other choice. At the time, my grandfather worked in the offices of the police station. He knew his entire family would be at risk of being killed if they didn't leave.

It takes strong and brave people to flee a country without knowing what's on the other side. When they first arrived in the US, they didn't have anywhere to go. So they retreated to a homeless shelter in downtown Los Angeles. It wasn't until a church provided them with temporary housing that they were able to begin their new life and move forward.

Both sets of my grandparents worked in factories most of their lives and faced great hardships. I admire their stories and hold them close to me, feeling the sacrifices they made for their families. The immigrant story is similar for millions of Hispanics in the United States today. It's a story of dedication and perseverance, and I share this with you because it's such an integral part of who I am and how my values were shaped. Knowing my family has endured and sacrificed so much for a better life gives me great appreciation for the opportunities we have today.

But as a Latina in the US, there are societal constructs, beliefs, and pressures that are felt differently as a whole than by the average American. As Latinas, we often feel silenced within our families because we aren't the patriarch. From a young age, one familiar saying told to young girls quite often is "calladita te vez más bonita," which means "you're prettier when you're quiet." Latina women were taught at a young age to be quiet and let the men do the talking. Our culture believes we are at our best serving the men in the kitchen and caring for children. Like many women, Latinas often assume the role of household managers, family caretakers, and mothers, in addition to being employees.[1] We continue to be seen as less valuable because our work doesn't take place in business; instead, it takes place domestically. And this has resulted in a drastically significant impact for us in the workplace.

Furthermore, in Latin households, women are taught to serve the men, as their needs are considered more important and should be met first. These societal beliefs are taught through actions as simple as chores around the house. For example, mothers teach young girls to make their beds and wash the dishes, but they refrain from teaching the boys these same chores. Boys aren't expected to do any of it. But why?

Today, seeing these societal traditions play out impacts how women see themselves in the household and in life. As Latinas continue living out a subservient lifestyle, men continue to live out their "machismo." Machismo is defined as "a strong or exaggerated sense of manliness; an assumptive attitude that virility, courage, strength, and entitlement to dominate are attributed or concomitants of masculinity."[2] Derived from the Spanish word *macho*, this term refers to the ideal societal role men are expected to play in their communities.

Though machismo is another word synonymous with

sexism and misogyny, it is also a strong and commonly held belief in Hispanic communities that men are genuinely superior to women for the benefit of the family, work, and society. This "role" assumes that the man is always seated at the head of the table, both figuratively and literally, to act as a protector of the family and to demonstrate dominance. On a societal level, the role of the macho functions as a collective group of dominating men in all spheres of life—from the employment force to ruling political and economic institutions.[3]

These familial and cultural ways being taught within our families hold women back. Imagine for a second the difference it would make if both genders were taught the same things. If you live in a household and eat at the dinner table, shouldn't both genders be taught to do household chores? Shouldn't both boys and girls be taught to load the dishwasher and fold the laundry? This habit for mothers to only expect and teach girls to do household chores is a form of perpetuating the machismo culture within Latin homes. Consequently, as they grow up, little boys become young men who then expect their wives to do the same for them. It's a cycle.

These stereotypes are damaging not only to women but also to the entire family. It can take years before they break out of this cycle of being at home to being fully independent. It is these moments in Latin families that cause us women to "go against the norm" and do something different. Now more than ever before, it is time we continue advocating for ourselves.

This problem for Latinas gets solved twofold: (1) with the support of government and businesses providing resources and programs for Latinas and (2) by Latinas practicing advocating for themselves, fully embracing their confidence and owning it.

According to a study done at UCLA, in order to help working Latinas reenter the workforce and maintain stable employment, we should be doing the following:

- Providing childcare subsidies and improving childcare quality, affordability, and availability
- Permanently expanding the Earned Income Tax Credit (EITC)
- Strengthening education and training programs to upskill Latinas[4]

Whether the issue is business or health care or government, we need to start advocating for ourselves, speaking up on our own behalf instead of waiting for someone else to do it for us or assuming we won't be heard. We were told to be quiet as Latinas, but now we must continue speaking up. The more in tune you are with your abilities, the better you can be at communicating what they are to the world.

It's interesting. So many times when I have tried to speak up and advocate for myself, it has felt hard to do because it feels as if I am being conceited or stuck up. But we can express what we are good at and stand up for ourselves in a humble and kind way. We need to continue practicing, myself included. The first couple of times you stand up for yourself or communicate your needs can feel a bit rocky because you might get some pushback or you may feel weird and uncertain doing it. But the more you practice, the better you get at it, and the more normal standing up for yourself and advocating for your abilities becomes. So just start! Whether it's your next job interview, your next rehearsal, your next big presentation, your next big idea, or whatever it may be, I want you to go in there and advocate. Not only for what you are working on, but also for yourself.

Within our homes as mothers, we need to advocate for both little girls *and* boys to learn how to do household chores. The saying "it starts at home" couldn't ring truer. If we start teaching these habits at home now, then we will continue to teach the next generation. After all, if we don't advocate for both genders to do the work at a young age, then who will?

Reframing and rewiring these cultural norms taught to us at young ages can help us remove these mental barriers that have been placed upon us. As Latinas, we are strong. We are passionate. We are dedicated and hardworking. We deserve to sit at the same table based on our capabilities, not our gender. And we will get there. It's time for us to practice living out our lives the way we wish the norms were structured. It won't be easy; it never is. But little by little, we will rise to power. And it's going to be amazing.

CHAPTER 6

DISCOVERING AND BUILDING YOUR PURPOSE

For years, we have seen men run organizations and companies down Wall Street with aggressive tactics and a deep need to kill the competition and set ablaze everyone in their path. We have seen men tear others down in meetings and push others straight to the top. We have seen them use ego to make bad decisions, and we have seen ego get in the way of their ability to see clearly and make decisions for the greater good of an organization. And this became the norm in society. It became normal to see men in Fortune 500 companies make decisions that ultimately led them to bankruptcy, financial distress, or legal problems. (Cue *The Wolf of Wall Street* and many others.)

And yet today, so many female CEOs are carving a new path entirely for women. One of the main reasons I am so drawn to Sara Blakely and learning about female business founders is because I am in awe of how they lead. It's clear that men and women have different leadership skills. But one of the things that I find most interesting is when women lead with their femininity. They ask how their employees are doing and take into account their employees' feelings. They provide mentorship, reassurance, and a sense of community for their employees. It's a culture set with a different tone. They care a great deal and deeply, something that comes so naturally to us, as we are emotionally in tune with those around us. And at the end of the day, they are just as successful monetarily, if not more so at times, than men are.

Sara created a solution for women. She would tell herself that she was going to create a product to help millions of women. And guess what? She did. In recognizing her strengths, she brought Spanx into reality and stayed true to herself, her silly and funny self. She never took herself too seriously and loved to bring humor and goofiness into her everyday life. And through it all, she listened to her intuition. She trusted in herself and knew she was meant to create something bigger than herself.[1]

Have you ever gone against that small voice in your head because someone told you they wouldn't need your presentation or because you believed someone who you had a fishy feeling about? Then after you missed an opportunity to pitch your business, you paused and thought, *Ugh, I knew it! I should have listened to myself?* I'm sure there are hundreds of times you can think of when you went against what your gut was telling you. And I'm sure you always ended up wishing you had paused and thought, *Okay, I hear you!*

This is women's intuition, the little voice or gut feeling that tugs at us before leaving the house, reminding us about our purse or to turn the hair curler off or to give the pitch despite what others have said. A woman's intuition is rarely wrong; it's our best asset. Your intuition will not steer you in the opposite direction; it's your compass and guide. The challenging part is listening to it, but the better we get at listening to it, the better we get at trusting ourselves and making better decisions in every aspect of our lives.

So many people will tell you what to do or how to do it. But the truth is the only person who can do that is you. Your gut and your intuition will make the best decisions. Coaches can only do so much. They can support you on your journey of self-discovery and in the work you do to get you there. They can be your cheerleaders and number one fans. They can pick you up when you're down on yourself.

But the realizations and deep life decisions are within you. At the end of the day, you are the only person who can make the best decisions for you. You're the only one who can do the work to uncover what those decisions are. And the same goes for making decisions at work. Often, we are forced to feel that choices can only be black and white, but it is a woman's greatest asset to evaluate situations through the lens of empathy in business.

Julia Boorstin, a CNBC correspondent and author of *When Women Lead*, explained this concept perfectly. Throughout her book she discusses how "women are more likely to include varied perspectives in decision making and as a result are better at empathizing with both colleagues and customers. They often lead with vulnerability, a willingness to ignore expectations and to do things their own way. Women frequently focus on achieving a greater purpose beyond profits and are more likely to pursue social and environmental goals with a heightened sense of gratitude for their access and opportunity. Their approaches may have been overlooked, undervalued, or not associated with leadership for the simple reason that it is women who most often exhibit them."[2]

Female leaders today are setting new examples and new societal norms for the way in which culture is set and values are lived out. They care more about the community they do business with. According to the Global Entrepreneurship Monitor, "In general, among the 50 economies participating in the 2019 GEM research, men tend to be more financially motivated in their objectives . . . than women. An interesting finding is that women are generally more purpose-driven than men. Women starting a business are more likely to agree with the motivation of making a difference to the world."[3]

The impact that businesses have on our communities is

becoming more apparent, and as companies, we have a responsibility to help those around us. Paul Sullivan writes in *The New York Times*, "Impact investments, which aim to promote a social good or prevent a social ill, have significantly outperformed traditional bets during the coronavirus pandemic. . . . Over all, 64 percent of actively managed E.S.G. funds beat their benchmarks versus 49 percent of traditional funds."[4]

Today, many female entrepreneurs want to tie a purpose to their businesses. There is a deeper "why" to the work they are doing. The way we can break down business is simple: Sell something, make money. If your income exceeds your expenses, you made a profit. The end. Yes, businesses have to make money to operate. But let's draw one circle bigger. Businesses provide a service—you create a solution; you create a profit; both can drive an impact. Ah.

You see, we are all human. We can feel emotions. We can be hurt or healed by another person. We feel these things because of another's actions. Businesses, companies, industries, and society all together can create good and bad. In this world, we are interconnected by the things we consume, the food we grow, the items we touch. All these products come in and out of our lives and impact us in one way or another. We have the power to create and be a part of something that impacts others for the better. We can ensure that our path is one that lights another person up instead of bringing them down.

At the end of your day, what would you rather be a part

of? Chances are the answer is simple. And it's one that we can continue to bring into large problems and issues in society at large. We are all connected; we all can make a ripple effect, so why not be a part of a positive one?

Naming Our Passions

A few weeks ago, I connected with a young woman named Alison through my mentorship program. She was a twenty-two-year-old from Chicago, wanting to build her own beauty brand. She invited me to her pop-up store, a tiny spot in an outdoor shopping mall. It was very cute, and I was impressed by what she had been able to put together at such a young age.

When we sat down, she started telling me about herself. She was raised in a Hispanic household with nine other siblings. She said she felt a bit lost, as her family couldn't support her. She went to community college, but she dropped out after a year because she felt that her teachers weren't providing the information she needed to know about her business. Instead, she took three jobs and saved up until she had enough money to place an order for her first inventory.

But the one thing she knew for certain was her passion for beauty. Since she was little, she would play dress-up and makeup artist with her grandmother. They would play for hours, putting on makeup with different brushes and in different colors. Those were her magical moments, ones that she wanted to preserve and share with others.

When she finished her story, I said, "Listen. Most people spend their entire lives wishing they knew what they were truly passionate about. Not only that but people are afraid to pursue what they are passionate about. I think you are braver and have more courage than most adults do." I said this genuinely.

A grin appeared on her face, and she said, "It's all I have."

"You are a hundred percent sure in your whole heart and gut this is your true passion?" She nodded, and without hesitation, I said, "Then go for it. With everything you've got."

In that moment, us meeting felt like fate. I knew exactly what to do. We were going to build out her business plan, but we were going to start from within. She told me everything about her business—what she liked, what she didn't like, and what she dreamed about. She told me about her current products and the problems that came with them. We went over ideas about her products and how we could market them. But throughout this meeting, one of the things that stuck with me the most was watching Alison in real time understand the power of her personal story.

I asked her, "When you think of your favorite product, you think of a specific person using it. So, what do you want women to think when they are using your products?"

"I want them to really love them. But I haven't given it much thought after that."

"What I see when I look at you and your products is an amazing story of a girl going after her dreams. Against all odds. And someone who has a deep passion for beauty products. I also see someone who might not know exactly how to share her story, because she doesn't have a signature product." Alison looked a bit confused, so I continued, "Well, in addition to your story and communicating your purpose, what is one item that you can really knock out of the park?"

Alison wasn't sure, so I asked her to imagine her top three signature products, the products her customers would come back for time and time again. Why? Because she would do those products differently. They would be what she would be known for, why customers would come to her store and not some convenience store down the street. Customers would also come to her store to support her.

With tears in her eyes, Alison thanked me for taking the time to talk with her and for believing in her.

I looked around her tiny pop-up store, filled with flowers and a bright sparkly wall made of paint and glitter, and I knew her business would take off. Then I gave Alison a big hug and told her I was excited to see her six months from now. I knew she had so much potential and that exponential growth was waiting for her. This was just the beginning. We all have moments of uncertainty, but with support from mentors and a community, we can do just about anything. We just have to know what we are passionate about.

Purpose: What Do You Want to Stand For?

What I have come to appreciate is that women lead with their own styles. They bring a certain flair and sunshine. And that should be embraced because being ourselves and collaborating with others in order to create is a gift. How do you want to lead with purpose? For me, it means leading with heart. Leading with a solution. Leading with authenticity. What does it look like for you? What type of leader are you? What part of purpose do you want to partake in? Studies show that building a business while also building a purpose makes profitable sense. And it will be women who lead those companies to the finish line.

Now, you may be wondering: Well, what if I don't know? Or what if it's just a passion of mine? Well, that can all be true. But in my experience, there is one more puzzle piece to discovering your passion: What is the most pain you've ever experienced in your life? Yes, you read that correctly, and yes, it's not fun to think about or even easy to read. But let me tell you one of my stories.

I found myself often on the floor, simply trying to figure out what it was that deeply impacted me. This question ate at me for months. I so badly wished the answer would just come to me magically in a dream. But nights came and went, and I was still purposeless. Even worse, I would feel silly seeing the people around me knowing their answers quickly and me not being even remotely close. Well, I had that feeling for months and even years, and all I could come up with was journaling, watching Netflix, and reading. Well, heavy on the Netflix and especially TikTok rot sessions on my couch . . . But really. How in the world are we supposed to know?

In true Alexis fashion, the moment of realization came to me on stage in a Q&A session. Someone asked me, "What was something painful you were able to overcome?" As I sat there and thought about it for a moment, it all came to me. That was exactly it. I told the story of a huge failure I had endured and of rebuilding my self-worth.

Stunned at my own realization, I took a moment to regroup. I looked over at the individual in the audience and responded, "Well, let me ask you the same question. Can you name a time that was painful and how you overcame it?" Because truly, that can and will define us as humans. How does someone get up after a failure? How does someone keep enduring pain repeatedly without giving up? How does one continue to go to practice day in and day out without throwing in the towel? Well, those are the answers that only we can answer. Because only *we* are the ones that went through that journey.

Anyone who has endured a true pain or failure can look back and describe in their own words how they got through. The series of events, thoughts, and moments that got them to the finish line becomes their very own playbook on "how to overcome." But it was then that I realized all past experiences truly happen for a reason. The pain I felt internally while the outside world kept spinning. The low moments of self-hatred, body shame, and lack of worth, all a part of something much bigger I couldn't see amid the pain and tears. Those nights alone, single, wondering what was wrong with me. And I sat there on stage in silence. It was now my very own playbook on how to believe in yourself. It was my playbook on how to rewrite your internal limiting beliefs. It was my playbook on how to rise above a heartbreak and find yourself. It was my playbook on how to turn pain into passion.

After healing myself, I had the playbook on how to build my self-worth and confidence. And now I have the opportunity to share it with the world. I have the keys to help someone else overcome a similar experience. After months of work, that became and was now clearly defined as my purpose. So, what is it that you have struggled with in your life? Because chances are, once you overcome it, you can help others overcome it too.

Think about it: Have you ever had a conversation with someone about a past pain and felt an immediate connection because they went through something similar? Well, that is the exact feeling that people will have when they hear about how you overcame a struggle. Because chances are they are feeling something similar. I wholeheartedly believe that we are called to cure and heal ourselves, because that is the key to how we will show up in the world to help others. If we can do it for ourselves, we become experts. We become lived experiences, all built together that equal your very own solution. And what good would we be if we didn't share it with others?

But here's the catch: I believe that your pain turns into your passion, which then turns into your North Star. It becomes your life's nonnegotiable, something that you are unwavering on and won't ever let happen to you or others again. What is that "change" or "issue" or "misconception" that you won't let others cross your boundary on? Spending so much time healing allowed me to understand the power you can have on others by sharing this North Star. It becomes the guiding principle for your life. For example, believing that every person deserves proper medical care, or the opportunity to start their own business, or to live freely from abuse or starvation. The list goes on, but whatever that North Star vision is for you, that driving force quietly hums within you throughout your everyday life.

So, are you ready to find your passion? If so, then look deep within, because somewhere in your past will be the answer, a lesson and a story that you can share with others.

EXERCISE: Turning Pain into Passion

Defining Your Strengths

- What are your strengths? (We have worked through this in previous chapters, so go ahead and insert those answers here, knowing you have identified them.)
- What are you good at? What do you enjoy doing that comes naturally to you?

Identifying Your Passions

- What are you personally passionate about?
- Write down your personal pitch for yourself: What do you have to offer?
- Say it out loud—did it feel and sound right to you? Are you confident in delivering that to someone?

Identifying Your Pains

- What have been your biggest struggles and challenges?
- What happened? Can you identify a specific moment or issue?
- How do you think you can bring forth something positive from this pain point? Can you think of a few things you could do to turn this into a lesson or help to others?

Finding Your North Star

- Where do your strengths, passions, and pains intersect?
- **Strengths + Passions + Pains = Your North Star**

See the following graphic for an example of my North Star.

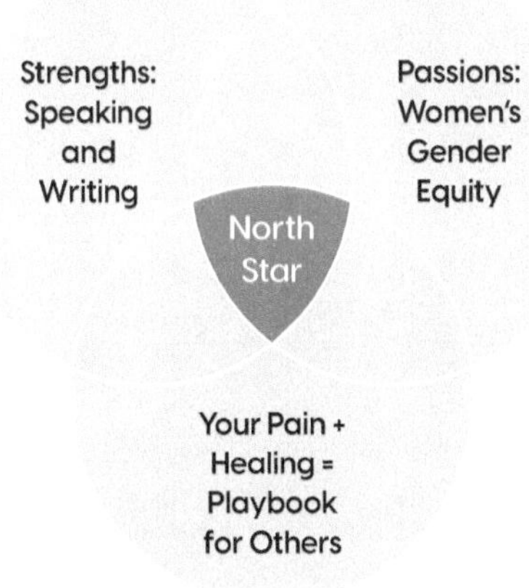

CHAPTER 7

THE IMPORTANCE OF MENTORS

Let's set the scene. Imagine you walk into your favorite local coffee shop during lunch. The espresso machine is on, the sounds of the milk frothing are loudly gurgling, and the classic jazz music is on in the distance. You believe that today is going to be great because you're going to be meeting and getting advice from one of your biggest inspirations and role models in your career. You've been a fan of this person for years, and you can't believe that you're going to meet them personally. You feel excited and giddy, and your adrenaline is rushing in. Your coffee arrives, and you take a sip. You quickly get your notebook and pen out and patiently wait for them to arrive.

The minutes go by, then slowly, a couple of minutes turns into thirty minutes. And then an hour later, your role model walks in, apologizes, and sits down. She is frazzled, wearing workout gear, and barely awake. She can't remember your name, doesn't know where you work, and makes you start telling your story from the beginning. Within seconds, your gut sinks to the floor. Your stomach is in knots because you are already so let down, and your gut is telling you it's only going to get worse. How could the one person you looked up to so much not know a thing? As time goes on, you realize your gut was right, and the meeting gets even worse.

She gives you generic advice, she doesn't take time to listen to your story or aspirations, and she gives you the same quotes that Pinterest generates. What just happened? This person didn't take the time to be professional or show you respect. But even deeper than that, it's the realization that she didn't make you feel special or heard. There wasn't a connection between either of you, and her lack of effort is not only disappointing but also hurtful. Ouch.

Can anyone relate? This scenario happens all too often. It's one that crushes our insides and reminds us that others have the power to disappoint us from what our expectations were.

This scenario has happened to me many times. In preparation for writing this book, I connected with a few individuals who I thought would be great to learn from. I was beyond excited to meet with them and ask them tons of questions about everything—how they got to where they are in their careers, what steps they took, what they went through, and so on. But instead of giving me the insights I was hoping for, they gave me the most generic answers possible. They put up the "perfect" personas and talked about their careers as if things were great 24/7. Every answer they gave was not the least bit relatable. The entire time I kept thinking, *Okay, but how did you REALLY do it?* I wanted the truth! Where were the ups and downs, the self-doubt, the insecurities, the voices telling you how big of a failure you were if you messed up? I left unimpressed, uninspired, and unmotivated.

Our role models and mentors can leave a big impact on our lives. In those moments of growth, we tend to seek someone to look up to for inspiration, a shining light, someone to tell us that we can keep going and that if they can do it, then so can we. But the reality is that it's our responsibility to be real. The women and role models who have made the biggest impact on my life were the ones who were real and authentically themselves. They were not only incredible leaders, but they were also incredible mentors because of their ability to be authentic in every aspect, both professionally and personally. And they cared. They truly, deeply cared about me and how they could improve my trajectory.

It is so easy to hide behind the monotonous response of "My job is incredible, and I love coming to work with my team every day" when you have been through a lot of insecurities and struggles the past week. There are so many ways in which we can turn and give honest lessons to our mentees, which is what is so desperately needed. When we do finally find that mentor who means the world to us, we need them to keep it real. And when we become someone's mentor, it is our responsibility to be real, to not give fluff answers and pretend like everything is great. Our responsibility is to ensure that we are coming to the table authentically as ourselves. The more honest we can be, the more we can develop real relationships and have a greater impact.

Knowing this, let's rewind and reset the scene. You walk into the same coffee shop. The espresso machine is on, the sounds of the milk frothing are loudly gurgling, and the classic jazz music is on in the distance. But instead of getting ready to meet your biggest role model and career inspiration, you are meeting a colleague from a different company. They aren't the person you've always been most excited to meet, but you think why not. It's nice to meet new people in your network. This person arrives right on time, addresses you by your full name, and sits down with a smile. They immediately ask you about yourself, your job, your passions, your day-to-day.

After half an hour, this person has really gotten to know you. They listened and heard you. They also asked questions about your passion and what you wanted to achieve. They took the time to listen to your story and give you feedback on how you can take the next steps in order to succeed. They told you not to worry about a specific scenario because they, too, had failed in the same situation. You had a real conversation with someone who is honest and forthcoming. You leave surprised and excited. Inspired. Moved. Heard. Seen.

The lesson is loud and clear: We need real, honest answers about who we are, including successes and failures. People want to be seen, heard, and valued, and listening to what someone has to say without judgment and with full empathy is the first step. We owe it to each other to share the truth of how we got to be women in positions of power. We can't continue to hold back the very stories that will inspire others.

My First Mentor

After I graduated from college, I started my career working at a food manufacturing and distribution company in their sales and marketing department. This position taught me how companies operate, how to get accustomed to a workplace environment, how to work in teams, and how to get projects done. I was uncertain when I began because I didn't know what I wanted to focus on. I had a lot to learn and felt a bit overwhelmed. But I knew that starting in one department and taking the time to sit in on meetings and absorb everything would be an amazing experience. I value the early days when I first started out because I could learn without fear of failure. I allowed myself to make mistakes, fall, and get back up. But the only reason I was able to feel comfortable doing so was because of my direct boss, Katherine. I'll never forget my first week on the job. I was sitting in my cubicle, going through marketing materials, and she came over to introduce herself.

"Hi, I'm Katherine!"

When I looked up, I saw a woman smiling from ear to ear. Her excitement was unlike how I'd ever been greeted before. She wore a bright blue suit and walked into the room with a burst of confidence and energy. Her warm and bubbly demeanor had a way of making people around her feel at ease. "Welcome to the office! We are so excited to have you!" she said as she guided me to her office.

As we walked in and I sat down, she excitedly expressed that they needed help in their marketing department. I knew I loved marketing and was ready to roll up my sleeves and help in any way possible. But after a few days getting to know each other, she stopped over at my desk and pulled me aside.

"Alexis, have you ever had an interest in learning about sales?"

"No, I haven't really given it much thought. I always had an interest in marketing and was going to focus on that," I responded politely, unsure of where this conversation was headed.

She smiled and said, "Fantastic. I know you had initially expressed interest in marketing, but after getting to know you and having you around for the past few days, I think you would be incredible in sales."

Sales? I thought. *Isn't that going to take a lot of preparation and practice?* I'd gone to school for marketing, but I'd never learned a thing about sales. (Mind you, I was twenty-two and had a limited understanding of different departments and their responsibilities.)

She nodded. "Alexis, I see something in you, and I think you should give it a try. You might not know it yet, but it might be something you end up loving even more."

My stomach was slowly turning inside out. Sirens were going off in my head, and I began to panic.

"I've never done it before, but I'm willing to try!" I said, trying to push my anxious feelings aside.

"Great, let's give it a start. I'll teach you everything you need to know. Trust me, you got this!" She pulled a chair next to me and slid the phone toward herself. She selected a few numbers from the directory, then pointed at a potential client and wrote their phone number on a yellow Post-it.

"All right, we are going to cold-call this person, and it's going to be great!"

I nodded back with a blank stare, a thousand questions running through my mind. What if they answered and she didn't know how to respond to their questions? We could lose a client, or worse, we could be known as the women who were unprofessional.

"Before you dial the number, I have a question. What if we don't know what to say? Or I don't know the answers?"

"Well, you are the expert! In sales, it's our job to know our product and company inside and out. And once you are the expert, there is nothing you won't know or feel comfortable talking about. They know nothing, and you know all the details. You know all the numbers, sizes, prices, and products. And if you don't, let them know you'll confirm and get back to them. It's all a part of the process," she said.

I immediately felt my anxiousness wane. Air started to come back into my lungs, and I took a deep breath. Okay, so it would take some time and practice, but after a while, I could become an expert. Suddenly, I heard her nails clicking the numbers of the phone.

Ring . . . Ring . . .

"Hello, this is James, may I ask who is speaking?"

"Hi, James, this is Katherine, how are you today?"

"I'm great."

"I'm with the Food Company that recently emailed you, and I wanted to talk about an opportunity to serve your customers. Do you have two minutes?"

"Sure, I'm in the process of looking for a new provider. What ya got for me?"

She proceeded to explain the company and what our services were in a quick but digestible way. With ease and sincerity, she told him everything he needed to know. And to my utter shock and surprise, by the end of the phone conversation, he had agreed to meet us in person to taste the product and learn more.

"It's been great talking with you, James. Alexis and I look

forward to meeting you in person in two weeks!" *Click.* And just like that, the call was over, and we landed a meeting.

Katherine and I stared into each other's eyes and squealed.

"I cannot believe you just did that! On your first phone call with him? How is that possible!"

She began laughing. "Look, it doesn't always happen that easily, but it's just an example to show you that it's possible. So, create your list of target customers, get their contact information, and just give them a call. Remember, people are people at the end of the day. And there's a group of people who are interested in at least trying what we have to offer." Nothing about what she had just done was complicated. In fact, I thought it was something I could do, maybe even successfully.

And from that moment, she took me under her wing and taught me everything she knew and had grown to understand over her career. She saw in me my strengths and recognized where they would shine. She was right about everything. I couldn't believe that she had just picked up the phone, cold-called, and landed a meeting. Unbelievable. She made it look *so* easy. I didn't know it then, but that day was the beginning of my love for sales, relationship building, and people. Because of her I learned a different aspect of business I never thought was an option for me. And little did I know that sales is a skill that you can use in any part of business, whether it's selling your own company as an entrepreneur, communicating your plan for a city, or expressing your perspective on a board. Sales is an integral part in making any business, organization, or nonprofit run. It's communicating your services to another.

Katherine had the opportunity to influence, shape, and impact a young woman starting out in her career, and trust me when I say I've never felt so inspired and deeply blown away by someone I've worked with. Her light shined so bright within every room, across every executive table, and inside every buyer meeting. She did everything with warmth, positivity, and grace. She never talked bad about anyone, and she always supported her team.

The best way I can describe Katherine as a whole is that she was in a constant state of effervescent positivity. The kind of energy that made it impossible for you to have a bad day, ever. No matter what business problem came up or issue we had to tackle, she would simply say, "That's okay, how can we fix it?" She gave everyone the reassurance that everything had a solution, no matter how difficult or tough things got. She leaned into her warm, caring, and loving qualities that she held strongly as a mother. She cared about her team deeply. They would follow her through any hardship, trusting that she would protect them and had their best interests at the forefront of her decisions. She was authentically herself and never let anyone change her no matter how loud her laugh was or how different people thought she was. But what was truly invaluable about working with Katherine was that she was a woman breaking barriers in every direction.

I look back with an overwhelming sense of gratitude and appreciation for the time I got to work with her. Having a boss and mentor like Katherine was a game changer for me. She set the bar and expectation for not only how I see other leaders but also for the standard that I hold myself to. She was irreplaceable.

Both my first-grade teacher and my first boss helped create defining moments in my life, for the better. I know that we as women can all have that kind of impact on someone else's life. And so, I challenge you to be that person for another young woman. When given the opportunity and when you see something in someone, say it. Give them those words of kindness or tell them that you see them for their amazing work. It will never go out of style, and it will always help bring another woman up. We need to continue to support all women on their journey toward being authentically themselves and confident in their abilities and strengths. If you can see it, you can believe it. Having a mentor in our lives helps to achieve goals we didn't think were possible, both professionally and personally.

The Need for Female Mentors

Andie Kramer writes in *Forbes*, "One study found that 87 percent of mentors *and* mentees feel empowered by the relationship and reported greater confidence and career satisfaction. And, it turns out that mentees *and* mentors are both promoted far more often (5 times and 6 times, respectively) than those employees without mentors."[1] This is a necessary and key component to moving forward and holding a position of power. Women with sponsors are more likely to ask for stretch assignments and pay raises than women without sponsors.[2] Having people advocate on your behalf allows you to gain credibility in the workplace and have others say your name in rooms when discussions of promotions come up. The more we can advocate for women to get into power, the more there will be for the next generation to look up to.

As women in our careers, there's nothing better than the feeling of knowing that someone else believes in you, that another person not only has your back but will also speak up for you in a boardroom setting and vouch for you. "The evidence is clear: 75% of executives credit their success to mentors and recent research shows that 90% of employees with a career mentor are happy at work," Christopher "CJ" Gross writes in the *Harvard Business Review*.[3] Whether it's through work or personal lives, role models and mentors are crucial for women along their path to achieving their dreams. These special mentors give us that glimpse of hope that we want to see in ourselves but sometimes can't. They see things in us that we can't see and allow us to stretch and achieve a little bit further than what we imagined for ourselves. The need for women to have role models is incredibly important.

If mentorship is such a crucial part of advancing in your

career and confidence building, why doesn't everyone have one? Why is it that women lack direct mentorship? A whopping 76 percent of people think mentors are important, yet only 37 percent have a career mentor. And of those, 14 percent of mentor relationships started by someone asking a person to be their mentor, while 61 percent of those relationships developed naturally.[4]

Wait a second, rewind for a moment. Not only is there a lack of mentorship for women but one of the least used options to get a mentor (by simply asking) is at 14 percent? How can this be? What is stopping us from reaching out and sending a simple email or picking up the phone? If the solution is so simple, why can't we improve these statistics? After learning about these statistics, I started to think back to my experiences trying to mentor young women.

During a conference in 2024, I was on a panel to discuss women in business. It was an exciting day, walking into the auditorium. I remember the energy buzzing through the room in anticipation for the events. I headed backstage and said hello to everyone. Fellow panelists, guests, and leaders were there ready to go. Walking on stage, I could tell there was a great group of women in the audience. As we started the conversation, so many great points were discussed. From equity and inclusion to work life balance and motherhood, the topics were integral to the conversations.

As the talk concluded, someone in the audience raised

their hand for the Q&A portion and asked, "Alexis, can you give some advice or guidance on how we can build better mentorships in business?"

"Wow, great question . . . well, to answer this, I am going to share a personal story with you. But the short answer to your question is don't be afraid to reach out," I said.

"Over the past few years, I connected with lots of young women and personally gave my card to twenty individuals. I let them know that they could reach me at any time for résumé advice, interview practice, or just to talk about an idea they have," I said. "But guess how many of them actually reached out to me?" I paused and looked out into the crowd. A few of them were shaking their heads, uncertain.

"Only *one*," I said with a sadness in my voice. The women went quiet. They were pensive, and so was I. It left me confused and a bit let down. Why is it that the other nineteen never reached out?

But as soon as I finished my sentence, I paused. *Oh my God*, I thought, and it hit me. I had done the exact same thing to one of my mentors. As the lights shined brightly on me, I just sat there. And in that moment, I had the real answer.

Then I began again. "If I am being honest with you all, ironically, I might have done the exact same thing myself. If you don't mind, I think I am going to share it with you all, because it might help you see that all women fall into this mentality, me included." I paused.

"I was introduced to an amazing female entrepreneur a few months ago. During the event, we really hit it off. We both had a lot in common, had similar backgrounds and stories, and I knew she would be someone I could learn a lot from. When the event was over, she stayed to catch up with me and gave me her business card. She said, 'You can reach me anytime you need advice or want to talk about work. Know that I am here for you however I can help.' Well, months have gone by, and I haven't reached out. There have been so many moments where I wished I could reach out and ask her a question but stopped myself from pressing send. And last week, our mutual friend that introduced us asked me if I had reached out. And my response to her?" Well . . .

"Because I keep telling myself she's too busy for me. I keep thinking she is running her own business, has five kids, a husband, and dogs, there is *no way* she has time for a call with me. And the other thing that's stopping me from reaching out? I keep thinking I don't want to bother her by texting or calling her. I don't want to disrupt her or disturb her because she must be *so* busy with everything going on. She might just laugh at my request. 'Are you crazy?' our mutual friend said. 'Alexis, you have to reach out to her.'"

Whoa, I thought. Did I just say that on stage out loud? Yup. I sure did. And that was my full 360 moment. It was the moment where I deeply knew and understood exactly why nineteen of the twenty young women never reached out to me.

Because we don't think people have time for us. Because we think they are too busy and too great and too big for us. We think there is no way they'll think we're important enough to put on their schedule. As women, we downplay ourselves. We don't want to interrupt or ask or make someone else change their schedule or routine for us. We already know how hard it is to balance everything like octopuses out of water.

So, I began again. "Those young women never reached out to me because it's scary. So many times, we meet an incredible person, but before sending them an email requesting a meeting or time to review their résumé, we immediately think they are too busy. We write it off and stop ourselves from pressing send because we don't want to bother them. But the truth is the reverse—seasoned women want to mentor younger women. So many times I have met young women and offered to mentor them. To spend time and review their interview questions, and yet no one reached out. I am lucky if I get one to text me to meet for coffee! And I have thought, *Why won't these young women reach out to me*? Something that I so deeply cherish doing for others yet have difficulty asking for myself.

"Please remember that mentorship is not a one-way street. It's equally a two-way street. When we ask for help and support, we are giving someone else an opportunity to help someone else, which is a gift. From the perspective of your future mentor, once this person builds their career and achieves their version of success, many times they realize that it's time to bring people along with them. No one can build anything alone. Much of bringing an idea or initiative to life is working and collaborating with others. So many times, we want and wish for something great. But at the end of the journey, we realize that it wasn't the actual outcome that was valuable, it was the journey alongside the team that made it happen."

I concluded the Q&A portion and stepped off the stage. There was a moment in me where I thought, *Did I take that too far? Was I too honest?* But the second those thoughts had entered my head, I turned the corner of the stairs and saw lines of women waiting to speak to me. *Oh!* I thought. *I guess it did resonate!* The advice was incredibly well received, and I received so many thank-you emails and notes about my talk. Many had known the feeling all too well and were holding out on contacting their dream mentor for those exact same reasons. We get nervous; we get scared; we don't want to bother them; we don't think we are worthy of their time. I got all types of responses and reasons why women weren't reaching out, and they ran the gamut.

But more importantly, the women got to see firsthand that everyone has the same feelings, myself included, that we tend to stop ourselves and think there is no way someone would have the time. But, when the roles were reversed, I kept asking where all the mentees were! So, at the end of the panel, I challenged all the young women that night to go home and email one of their dream mentors and see what happened.

So, this is my challenge to all you readers: I want you tonight to draft an email to the most amazing mentor you've dreamed of having and reach out. WHY NOT? Chances are, no one else has done it. And according to the data, only 14 percent have! So, you've got yourself some great odds. Do it!

You Have a Mentor. Now What?

You got the mentor! They are also *incredible*! This person has experience in your industry and line of work, and you feel like you can grow a long-term relationship with them. AMAZING!

But the work doesn't end there. That's when your relationship and growth begin—surprise! Having a mentor is no different than having a relationship with someone, and relationships take work. If you want your mentor to introduce you to your biggest inspiration or write a letter on your behalf, you have to show them that you are worth it. Your work, your dedication, and your drive are all important factors in showing your mentor that you not only mean business but that you are also a credible person. Here are a few key things you can do to grow your relationship:

1. **Set a reminder to talk monthly or quarterly.** Depending on how busy your mentor is, it is critical that you create a constant flow of conversation. Remember, she

can't help you or guide you if she doesn't know what's going on. Take the initiative, coordinate times that work for the both of you, and schedule the meetings. If your mentor is busy and tells you, "Let's circle back and meet after the summer," you better set a reminder to reach out come September. Make sure it's on the calendar, otherwise things in our lives will get busy, and chances are you will both forget.

2. **Prepare, prepare, prepare.** Before your meeting, take the time to prepare. If there's a goal you want to achieve, make sure you have already done all the background research to understand what it will take to get there. Know what the qualifications and requirements are for your new position, know who the key players are in the industry you want to create your product in, and so on. It would be a shame to waste your time or hers just trying to understand the basic landscape when it could have been done at home. Google is your best friend! Use it. And now with ChatGPT and other AI platforms, there are so many resources at your fingertips to really dig in and become an expert.

3. **Make your goals crystal clear.** If you can't communicate your goals, how can someone help you achieve them? It's important to ensure that you have done the deep dive internally to know what it is you want to

achieve. Is it a super big goal like sitting on a corporate board? Is it getting your next promotion? Is it switching teams but you're unsure how to do so? Is it getting feedback on your entrepreneurial idea for a new product? Is it creating your own company? Whatever it is that you want to achieve, be ready to clearly communicate it in one to three sentences.

4. **Enjoy the process.** Your mentor decided to be your mentor for a reason. Chances are she sees a bit of herself in you—an eager and young go-getter who wants to go after her goals. And nothing is more exciting than the opportunity to help a young woman achieve her dreams, especially if you have the experiences and connections to help. Remember: Mentorship is a two-way street. It is enjoyable and fulfilling for both parties, so don't feel like you must hold back your questions or not get to know her personally. Some of my best relationships grew over time, and I got to know their greatest achievements while also learning about their greatest failures. Both are equally valuable but one sometimes harder to admit.

CHAPTER 8

"MOTHERS" AND GLINDAS

Now, as much as I want to believe and tell you that every mentorship is an amazing experience, sometimes it doesn't go as planned. And that's okay! Believe it or not, sometimes when people come into our lives and intentionally or unintentionally put us down or make us feel bad, it is a reflection of them, not of ourselves. Although these moments can be painful, they can help you see yourself more clearly. You are the only one who can allow someone else to make you feel bad. I bring this up because I want to share an important lesson that I learned when a relationship didn't go as planned.

With age comes great wisdom, which also brings a responsibility for us to mentor and support the next generation coming behind us. Women must stop putting down other women. When I say we need to be each other's champions, and when you hear the rhetoric in everyday social media and workplace environments, we truly mean it. It's one thing to say it, but it's another thing to live it and embody it.

Mentorship also requires us to work selflessly for the benefit of a young woman. Our time spent with them and the advice we give might not generate physical returns, but the emotional returns are tenfold and impactful. The most successful mentors and coaches are the ones who remove their own egos and narratives from situations and listen to their mentee's perspectives. Mentors listen and get down to the details of what it is their mentee wants to achieve, build, or grow. At the end of the day, the most successful mentors and coaches are the ones who focus on supporting that person to get to wherever it is *they* want to go.

A mentor–mentee relationship is very special and one that should be supported by positivity and kindness. I want women to know the power their words can have on a young woman with aspirations and dreams. Your words are critical and can make or break her spirit, which in turn can be damaging to her confidence.

There is a clear difference between giving someone feedback and criticizing them, so I want to provide some context behind the two. When someone is sharing their idea with you, you can either provide them feedback or tell them that their idea stinks. And there is a clear distinction. Giving someone feedback on their project, work, or idea can help them grow to the next level. When given correctly, it can be a huge asset for that individual to develop and improve themselves. For all mentors reading this book, I want to give a quick and easy outline for you to remember the next time you meet with your mentee.

1. Have your mentee's best interests at heart.
2. Provide solutions.

First, before sharing your thoughts, it is *so* important to remember to have that person's best interests at heart. Having someone's best interests at heart also means that you are kind and mindful with the tone of your delivery. It isn't always easy to be on the receiving end of feedback about how you can improve. But if given with kindness and thoughtfulness, your relationship and trust can grow stronger afterward. Starting off with a positive and kind response to the project or idea they shared with you is important because, the truth is, putting yourself out there is hard. And everyone needs support along their journey!

Second, there is so much value in providing solutions, not only your thoughts. When you come to the table ready to provide feedback, it's not about telling that person, "Oh wow, amazing, love it and can't wait to see more." It's about providing specific solutions on how to improve, grow, or become better. I want to share some examples that I have had directly with my mentees.

Catherine expressed her interest in launching her own website and asked me to look it over and give her feedback. After reviewing the website, I expressed how impressed and excited I was reading through it. I told her that the level and caliber of design she put into it were extremely well thought out. In terms of providing solutions, I started by asking her two questions: (1) Who is your target audience for this website? (2) How are they going to learn about your website in order to reach out to you?

She told me she hadn't thought about either of those questions, so we walked through some solutions and next steps. We discussed coming up with a target audience, building an advertising strategy on social media, and preparing content for her to share to get the word out. We also talked about a solution, which was including her website on her socials and business cards as well as a newsletter announcement about her website launch.

As a result, she walked away with tangible solutions to some of the problems she hadn't thought of yet. And best of all, I know that after she implements those solutions, her website is going to be better and will grow to the next level.

That is what we all want for our mentees—tangible solutions through feedback that can improve their overall idea. Which is very different from simply critiquing or criticizing someone by telling them that their idea stinks or that you don't think it will be successful. Hearing such negativity doesn't do anything for the mentee. It only puts them down and makes them doubt whether they should even try in the first place.

Everyone has to start somewhere, and most of the time, they have to start small. It starts at your kitchen counter or with friends and family and your community coming to support your first kickoff event. With effort, dedication, vision, and hard work, things grow and come together. It's all a part of a journey, one that most women have doubted and held themselves back from taking for so long. One that we, especially as women, cannot stop others from achieving. A win for one of us is a win for all of us.

Our "Mothers"

I like to say that "you always remember the people who cheer you on in life." As an executive who oversees Corporate Social Responsibility, my job is to ensure that we are growing the good in business by lifting up the communities and underserved populations around us.

I recently put on an event in partnership with a local nonprofit in Las Vegas and called it Women's Leadership Day. We invited more than ten young women from this nonprofit to attend an executive luncheon, where they each got to sit down and learn about the everyday life of an executive in business. These young women currently are recipients of a full scholarship at their university, as they applied and got accepted through their academics and family need. With the average family household earnings of these attendees being $30,000 a year, they qualified to become recipients, and with that also gained a one-on-one career mentorship throughout their college experience, setting them up for access post-graduation.

At the lunch, I led the young women and the executives on a challenge to step outside their comfort zones. I dared them to take the phone of the person sitting to the right of them and add themselves on their LinkedIn, to draft an email to their dream mentor and send it on the spot, or to stand up and ask a question they were secretly afraid to ask. The young women were scared at first, but by the end of the day, they started to trust the process and see how much they had grown in just a few hours.

The idea to host this event came to me when I was in a one-on-one coaching session with a mentee of mine and she shared what it was like growing up without her mother. Hearing the deep loss in her made my heart break in half, and I wanted to do everything I could to help her and provide her support. But hearing her story, I realized that even though many young women may have mothers, they might not have received the guidance or support they needed along the way. So when it came time to start the session on the Leadership Day, I began by telling them a quick story.

First, I asked the group whether anyone knew what the term "mother" meant for Gen Z. A few of the young girls quietly giggled, but the female executives silently shook their heads. "Well, I want to read to you what the ChatGPT definition of it is." So I took out my phone and read this:

To Gen Z, **"mother"** (often stylized as **"MOTHER"** in all caps) has evolved into a **slang term of high praise**, particularly within pop culture and internet communities. It's used to describe someone—usually a woman—who is iconic, influential, or unapologetically themselves in a way that inspires admiration, often for their style, power, authenticity, or cultural impact.

Here's what **"mother"** means to Gen Z:

A term of reverence and admiration

Think: *"She's MOTHER"* = *She's everything. She's iconic. She's untouchable.*

Used for cultural icons or trendsetters

Example: *Rihanna is MOTHER for showing up pregnant at the Super Bowl and still delivering a performance.*

Represents power, originality, and unapologetic confidence

It often implies someone is leading the way or breaking boundaries—just like a mother figure would in a metaphorical sense.

Examples in use:

"Beyoncé just dropped her visuals. She's MOTHER."

> *"You're serving looks today—very much mother."*
>
> *"She mothered so hard with that speech."*
>
> It's playful but deeply complimentary—think of it as a modern-day crown worn by those Gen Z sees as cultural royalty.[1]

As soon as I finished reading, a burst of laughter broke out in the room. The girls were smiling and many of the executives were laughing. I continued as the room fell quiet, and I asked them another question. "When we think of the ultimate form of mentorship, it's really someone you admire in all categories, right? Someone that is passionate, successful, kind, all the things important to you. So, who is someone you think is 'MOTHER' and why?"

Ultimately, as the girls started sharing, I realized that "MOTHERS" came in all different forms and people. They listed individuals from their aunties to Taylor Swift and Carrie Underwood to their sisters and their best friends. These individuals were their number one supporters, someone they could go to for advice, or someone they could look up to.

It was one of the best activities I could have ever done for the young women. They realized that everyone had someone different they looked up to in that sort of way. They also recognized that regardless of your family situation, you will always have people in your corner; you just need to find them.

MY MOTHER

Do you remember Glinda the Good Witch from *The Wizard of Oz*? She wore that light pink fluffy dress, sparkly shoes, and a beautiful silver crown and wand. No matter from what angle you saw her, she was glowing. A pink essence of sparkles, grace, and beauty all wrapped into one. She was a powerful sorceress in the Land of Oz and first appeared to Dorothy in a rainbow bubble. She helped Dorothy on her journey getting to the Emerald City successfully. In the end, when tested by the Wicked Witch of the West, she replied, "Be gone, you have no power here." Coincidentally, that is one of Oprah Winfrey's favorite lines.

Glinda was the original "mother." In *The Wizard of Oz*, the OG mother took care of her own power but also allowed for power to be recognized within others. Her energy was full of grace and her presence stood for peace among the town. She represented a woman in power who granted good, who believed in the goodness of others, and who wanted to bring the goodness out in everyone.

Glinda was also a teacher. If I had to make a modern-day comparison, I would equate her to the high priestess in the tarot deck of cards—someone who is here to serve, brings selflessness through listening and communication, and restores balance on the planet. An expert in their field, and someone who helps to heal and aid others around them. Someone who provides their guidance through their selfless support, presence, and advice. In my life, I have a real-life Glinda the Good Witch. I have the one person who kept me going through the ups, downs, and darkest times. I consider this person to be my secret weapon. The one superpower I always knew I had in my back pocket. My mother.

Growing up in Cuba, she came from humble beginnings. After moving to the US, her family didn't have much, but she always found happiness playing with dolls or styling and cutting hair. After childhood, she became a first-grade teacher. I grew up watching my mom in the classroom and visiting her classes. I don't think I realized I was living with my very own Glinda until I got into high school. I always knew she was wonderful, but the older you get, the more you realize and understand yourself as a human and an individual as well as those around you.

What I came to recognize about my mom as a person was that she had this ability to bring grace into every room she stood in. It was a magical ability she had because no matter the situation, she stayed the same. She stayed neutral whenever there was conflict and always saw the positive in every situation. She continually brought her light and positivity into our everyday life experiences. When we were sad, she would talk like Daffy Duck in a rustled and squeaky voice, and within seconds, laughter would erupt. When we were having a hard time, she would remind us that it's easy to fall apart, but it's harder to stay together. And that has rung true for me throughout my life.

It's easy to give up, call yourself a failure, and stay home. It's easy to throw in the towel, say you quit, and play the victim. But it takes bravery and courage to stand up the next day and keep going, to ask for help and recognize that you are not okay. To call that person you had a disagreement with and sit down with them to figure out a solution that you both agree on. To attend a meeting with the person who publicly humiliated you. To show up when you *really* don't want to. But with time, you can, and you will be okay.

But the one quality that allowed my mom to be the true good witch was her ability to show and give unconditional love. It's a superpower that goes beyond any ability. It's a quality that can't be quantified, only felt deeply. Her pure love is what has allowed me to experience total acceptance. And it's a feeling I hope to continue passing on to everyone around me. It's a feeling I hope all women give to each other, even in small doses. The way that we show up for the women in our lives is one of the most special things we can do for one another.

So many times in life we don't tell the people we love the most how we feel. I've seen so many tragedies where parents leave too soon, and children always wish they had one more moment to tell their parents something. Moments like these make me wonder how many times I tell my mother how much

I adore her. So, this is my wish for all of you. Take a moment and reach out to your Glinda the Good Witch. Tell them the one thing you wish you would have if they were gone. Because so many times we know what we would say but don't say it. And it's one of our biggest regrets.

I know not everyone grew up with mothers. I know many mothers have left this earth too soon. I know others were abandoned or don't know their mothers personally. But please know this: Regardless of your situation, there are hidden Glindas all around you just waiting to be your "mother."

MY HIDDEN GLINDA

When I was a little girl, my first-grade teacher gifted me a journal. It was bright red, and she had wrapped it in bright crinkly cellophane paper. She had read a few short stories I had written and took an interest in seeing them brought to life.

There was a short story specifically about two siblings who entered a magical world and, through their adventures in the caves, found the magic light treasure. But instead of telling me they were silly, which is what I had feared, she told me she wanted to read more. When she gave me the red journal, I opened it and found an envelope containing a letter she wrote. It read: "This is a place for you to continue to write all of your stories in." It was one of the best gifts ever given to me, but it wasn't the actual journal that meant a lot; it was knowing that someone believed in me. **That someone thought my stories were worth reading.**

One of the biggest lessons I've learned in my career is that female role models and supporters can be deal-breakers, tearing you down into pieces, or dealmakers, helping you become the person you have always wanted to be. When I was little, my first-grade teacher was a dealmaker to me. She saw me for my passion and recognized me for my work, and I never forgot it. My first boss, Katherine, was another role model and supporter who completely changed my life for the better by seeing strengths in me that I couldn't see for myself.

There are women on this earth who are here to support you and root you on. There are mentors, aunts, friends, and teachers who are here to show you the power you have within yourself. There are so many women who want to help other women. You just have to find them.

The Super Support Bench

One night on my way home from work, I was down. I felt like I had failed in a meeting, and I was being hard on myself. I didn't feel like calling my friends or family for support on it and instead found myself wallowing in my pain on the couch. My very own pity party was filled with candy and *Real Housewives* reruns. Perfect. (Raise your hand if you can imagine this and know exactly what I'm referring to.) But this isn't what got me off the couch and back up on my feet. Instead, I wondered whether there was something I could do to regulate my emotions, decompress, and get back on track.

Wouldn't it be great if I could build a support bench of people at home? Or have some sort of friendly reminders to look at or read whenever all other options were out? How could I create a place or something to help me get back up when I am down? I got up and grabbed a picture frame and my scissors and got to work. I printed out tons of photos, started grabbing mementos and items around the house, and brought them to a shelf at the top of my bookshelf that I had cleared off. I also grabbed old bulletin boards from my closet and put them on the table next to magazines and tape. Piece by piece, I started building a physical team and bench of supporters. When you visualize my support bench, imagine the top of a library shelf that holds a few different objects. I wanted each item to be significant enough to make me feel deeply. I had to connect with each piece because it had to work.

The first thing on the left-hand side of the shelf is a picture of my mom. She's that person who always told me, "You got this! Keep going. Don't give up." Every time I doubted myself, I had the urge to pick up the phone and ask her, "Are you sure that I should do this?" or "Are you sure I can make it?" She is my self-doubt squasher. We all need someone to believe in us.

Next is a stack of books that I look to pick up whenever

I need to be reminded how inspired I was by a person's story (Nicole Walters, Melinda French Gates, Jacqueline Novogratz, Eli Rallo, Tinx, Marie Forleo, Gabrielle Bernstein, Anna Kloots, Diane von Fürstenberg, just to name a few). I have come to love and find admiration for all these writers for their honesty and the way they are able to express themselves and their stories for others to benefit from. All of them are so different and yet made such a profound impact on me. These books made me feel seen.

There are photos of my closest friends and mentors, moments that immediately make me smile. Just looking at the photographs, I can hear their words: "You got this!" I printed a photo of Sara Blakely with one of her mug photos and another of her wearing her red backpack. These photos make me remember that it's possible to be a mom who stays true to herself and who is also successful. Next are photos of friends and special moments in my career, including the first time I spoke on stage and my first trip to visit a friend in Europe.

Your best friends, family, and coworkers are some of the best supports you can have in life. Your truest friends are the ones you can call at 3:00 a.m. and know they will answer. They see the greatness in you, even when you don't. After a quick coffee chat or call with one of these people in my life who has my back, I know I can get through another day. Best friends also help you see a different perspective and side to things. Their perspective can make whatever you are going through seem a little bit less painful when viewed through a different lens.

Next to the photographs is a stack of journals. Some are new and ready for new stories, while some are used, every page written on and rugged around the corners. Journals always help me write out the words that feel like a scrambled egg inside. Writing forces me to sit down and articulate whatever it is I am feeling as I put the words on the page. Journaling also allows me to imagine without restraint, to just let the words flow freely and each train of thought to come alive without judgment. Journaling provides a sense of calm, another outlet of peace in the craziest of times.

And as you near the end of the shelf, you will find a candle that was gifted to me. Its smell always makes me feel calm and also reminds me that the answers to any of my problems can be found within my intuition. We as women innately know what the answer is; we just need to be still and listen to what our gut is telling us.

My challenge for all of you is to find some time this weekend to go home and build your own bench. Fill it with whatever mementos and memories will bring you back to those positive feelings of believing in yourself. Your very own cheer squad and cheer team right at home! When you put together your bench, be thoughtful; you want it to evoke emotions of happiness, love, positivity, support, and so on. Things that make you smile and immediately take you to a place of pure joy. This is the place that provides a gentle reminder that you got this and to keep going. No matter what might happen, whether it is something as big as feeling scared you might lose your first election as a Latina mayor or as small as not wanting to get back up on stage after you mispronounce a word. In these moments when you come home, after you cry, dry your tears, and find your chamomile tea, I want you to walk yourself over to your support bench and remember, "I got this."

PHASE III

RISING TO LEAD: ACHIEVING YOUR GOALS, LANDING YOUR DREAM CAREER, AND STEPPING INTO POWER

CHAPTER 9

REDEFINING SUCCESS WITHOUT A RING

I've been single for so long I know every rule in the dating playbook. I have a go-to date outfit and the perfect bag to match. I know the rules of dating, and I can spot the red flags. I know the signs of a good and a bad date, the dates that will go down as a top ten worst, and the dates that will break you. I know what it feels like to be ghosted by someone you thought would be great, and I know what it's like to ghost someone who was excited about me. I know what rejection feels like, and I know what it feels like to reject someone else. So, hear me when I say, finding someone who I click with seems like climbing Mount Everest. It feels like I've tried every path and every route, and at this point, it's no longer in the cards for me. It feels like it's a game where I have all the right cards, but I'm playing with the wrong deck.

I spent most of my high school, college, and entire twenties dating, trying to find the one. My intention was clear: date to find my husband and win the game. I was naive and strongly influenced by everyone around me. I would go on dates but never really felt like things clicked. I would pretzel myself into whatever person I thought my date would want, but I was never truly myself. I kept my guard up high and my boundaries even higher. The older I got, the more I found that none of it was working. I felt empty and tired. I didn't want to win the game anymore, and I accepted defeat.

Then one day, I met someone through a mutual friend and took it as the sign I had so desperately been waiting for. After our first date, I genuinely felt like he was it for me. The perfect partner, the person who would quiet all the people asking how my dating life was going. Imagining our life together was my favorite thing to do because doing so gave me a sense of peace and relief knowing that my life, future kids, and history were ready to be set in stone. It also gave me a reprieve from the relatives and friends questioning why and how I could possibly still be single. The tensions and pressures started to melt away.

But when I expressed my hopes for our future together, they weren't reciprocated. Instead, they were thrown back at me with confusion and disgust. Rather than being my solution, it felt like my biggest failure. I'll never forget the deep pain of rejection, as if someone had destroyed my hopes and dreams, shut the door, and left me without a manual or guide as to how to proceed. My pain cemented me to the floor for multiple nights, unable to find the energy or way out. I couldn't imagine having to do it all over again, having to spend another decade single, waiting and wishing for a solution that would silence the deafening questions of why I wasn't good enough.

But that moment wasn't only about heartbreak; it was about something much bigger. It represented this idea and belief I had in my head that finding your true love and partner in life signified you won the game. That finding your significant other in life was the best day of your life. So many people, movies, novels, and stories have fed women this belief. Society has told us that no matter how successful you are in your career, there will always be something not good enough or missing simply because you are single.

Looking back, I couldn't have been further from the truth or more wrong about everything. Finding my way up off the floor allowed me to dig deep and find the truest form of courage. It allowed me to reach out to every one of my girlfriends and find a support system so strong I didn't realize it existed. I spent months rebuilding, growing, and getting back up slowly, day after day. I spent those days and nights alone, the ones that many people stay in bad relationships for. It was the most valuable time I have spent working on myself by reevaluating and rewriting the beliefs I had. As time went on, something was unleashed inside of me: the deep knowing and realization that I was not broken; instead, I was unbreakable. And my real story was just beginning.

The morning after we broke things off, I woke up and time stood still. Looking up from the floor, I saw the sunlight come through the window. I had cried so much that the entire front of my T-shirt felt like I had just mopped up a drink that had spilled on the floor. I don't remember much of the day, other than feeling numb. And quite honestly, feeling numb was better than feeling the immense sadness that had come earlier. I couldn't get myself to say it because I didn't want to believe it had happened or that it was true. But as I replayed that night in my head, I could see him shaking his head and turning cherry red. He had just admitted that he didn't see a future with me, and I was completely blindsided. Reliving the pain of embarrassment hurt more than it had in the moment.

My mind has a cruel way of making me believe the worst of every situation, and in that moment, I allowed it to. I felt like I should be punished for being so stupid. My mind raced. *You're such an idiot. He would never end up with you. How could you think so highly of yourself? You are worthless.* Those thoughts screamed louder as the day went on. How could I have misinterpreted everything and been so wrong? The hours lost in conversation, the eagerness to see each other again, the moments of finishing each other's sentences when we were together. I never pictured it any other way than us being together. It just made sense. It aligned. We aligned. I couldn't stop crying. The longer I stayed on the floor, the more normal it felt. But deep down, I knew it wasn't normal. In fact, it was far from normal.

It took days to slowly put myself back together and feel like a human again. As embarrassed as I was of what had happened, I never thought talking about it would end up saving me in the end. I reached out to my friends, and one by one, they picked up the phone and let me cry my eyes out until the tears stopped. Each one of them took the time to listen and provide their perspective, which were all different and each so valuable to my own healing process. Piece by piece, call after call, they helped bring me back to life. I truly thought that person had been the one, that we were destined. Hours and months spent together—it was the end game. But now, I realize that the entire quest to finding love was never a game.

It was the journey I needed to take to find myself.

It wasn't so much the loss of our relationship I was grieving, but the loss of the idea and expectation to be married at a young age. I was so focused on achieving that goal that I lost sight of what mattered and what was best for me. Not achieving that goal felt like failure, something I couldn't recover from. After I turned thirty, there was no going back. No magic pill to turn back time and ensure I didn't become a . . . pumpkin? What was I so afraid of? What if I could reimagine what success looked like? I started to think about what success would look like on my own terms. Instead of being married, what if

I could become an entrepreneur or sit on a national nonprofit board for women? What if I could advocate for young women on a national level? I let my thoughts wander; I allowed myself the time to think about what it was that would make me happy.

Without limitations or outside expectations, I started to see my future a little more clearly, one where I could envision myself becoming an artist and taking up painting. Having a studio in my garage is something I had always wanted but never gave myself permission to have. Or learning how to become the best professional speaker I could be. I could take the time to improve those skills and use them to connect with women. And in order for those dreams to come true, I had to be in the best shape mentally and physically that I could be.

I imagined what it would be like to have a healthy relationship with food and my body. No more negative and hurtful thoughts about my appearance, just living at peace with my body and my health. Now those were things I could get behind. Those were the images I had of myself and what being successful in life would be for me. Where in those images did getting married define my happiness?

The pain I felt after losing what I thought was my perfect partner was crushing. It was a mix of rejection, embarrassment, and failure all wrapped into one big sinking feeling that grounded me to the floor in a pool of tears. But looking back now on that heartbreak, I realize that it brought me clarity. It forced me to start picturing a life on my own and imagine things differently. When I got back up, I could see myself in a whole new light, and I knew who I wanted to be. That heartbreak allowed me to break free from seeking someone else's definition of success. It forced me to create my own definition of success:

Success is not finding your perfect partner.
Success is finding yourself.

Relationships can come and go. Love can come and go. Business partners can come and go. But the relationship you have with yourself is forever. The things you tell yourself every day when you wake up, the things you believe about yourself, how you treat yourself—those are the things that impact your relationship with yourself, which is the most valuable relationship you have in this lifetime. Investing in yourself is the best investment you can ever make. It's a guaranteed investment that will reap rewards and create a return.

I've come to realize that there is a big disconnect between what we want for ourselves and how we feel about ourselves. As women, we have been trained to always feel incomplete, to believe that we are never fulfilled or happy on our own, that we are less than if we don't have kids and a white picket fence. These inequities and narratives in our society are things we cannot control, but we have the capability of creating our own narrative. Our beliefs must come from within, not from peers, society, movies, or social media. We must hold strong and true for ourselves. We must not shy away from our female instincts, gut feelings, and intuitions, for those are some of our strongest powers. That belief in yourself will define who you become and what your career will turn out to be. That belief will set you apart from everyone else.

Although this may seem counterintuitive, I hope that every woman gets to experience heartbreak because what happens after is the magic portal to true transformation. That pain you feel can ignite into something much bigger than what you thought or imagined for yourself. Through heartbreak, I found myself. The younger girl who wondered what it would feel like to be strong on her own now knew. I no longer needed to rely on or wait for someone else to give me that power. The voices of society telling women they are falling behind and failing because they don't have a husband and kids at a certain age are and remain crazy.

I want us to start celebrating women for their achievements and reaching their goals with the same validation and applause society gives us for getting married or having kids. The amount of pressure, emphasis, and focus that people put on women's abilities to get married versus reaching their personal passions is not only unhealthy, but it is also very unbalanced. It gives the power and strength to something that, in reality, does not define you and, as statistics prove, might not last.

But your personal passions in this life deserve the same amount of value. Don't fall into the validation trap of marriage and kids. Do it because you want to, not because of the pressure society or others put on you. Release those pressures and focus on yourself: your dreams, your passions, what lights you up. Celebrate and emphasize your achievements and your personal pursuits of your dreams rather than having a white picket fence with kids and a husband.

Men continue to come and go in my life, but nothing has felt like home. And that's okay. I don't believe love is something you can force. People keep asking me what was wrong with the guy I last dated, but I can never explain it. My response? I just knew. It was just a feeling; something was off. I can't quite explain it. I had a gut feeling, one that I'll continue to listen to and bet on for the rest of my life.

Because the truth is, no one else can feel love for you. No one can be in your relationship or experience what it's like. You are the only one that has that capability. You are your best friend. You know yourself best. And if something feels off, kindly end things and move on. It's not fair to waste either of your time if deep down you know it doesn't feel right. What's more powerful or loving than putting your intuition and gut first?

In the future, I am open to love, marriage, and kids. But the one thing I won't budge or negotiate on is losing myself. When I've felt most at peace and excited about working toward my goals is when I defined my purpose in this lifetime. Without the judgment or pressure from anyone else. And that's when the magic happened. After I dug deep and really defined what success looked like to me, the real work began. Rebuilding from the ground up. The second I showed my vulnerability, I found my power.

The more real we are, the more leaders share that they have thoughts of not being good enough and questioning themselves. The more honest and transparent we are, the more the next generation of women can see us and believe that they can do it too, that they can be a leader. Women at any age are powerful, brilliant, and able to be fully whole on their own. Relationships don't define us; we define ourselves. The strongest and happiest women are the ones who have figured out how to be financially independent, fulfilled, and complete on their own. Finding the light and true joy in what we bring to this earth through our creativity, leadership, and talents is the best gift we can give to ourselves. My ability to create an impact in this world, feel fulfilled, and give my love to the people around me is my definition of success, and it's more than enough.

EXERCISE: What Is Your Definition of Success?

Put all the comparisons—to people on social media, in the workplace, or at school—away in a box for a few minutes and allow yourself to really think about it without any limitations or fears.

Someone might believe that being successful is owning a bakery and seeing customers come in and out every day with smiles. Someone else's success could be creating a solution for education. At the end of the day, success should be defined by everyone individually. Dig deep and redefine what it means to you.

- What goal or goals would make ME so proud of myself?

Think about these things for a few minutes before writing them down. Let yourself dream for a while.

- List out five life goals that would make YOU proud:

    - ______________________________
    - ______________________________
    - ______________________________
    - ______________________________
    - ______________________________

CHAPTER 10

COMMUNICATING YOURSELF AUTHENTICALLY

When it comes to personal branding, we have all heard the phrase "The most important brand you will ever market is yourself." And I totally agree; those words couldn't be truer. But the question is, are you brave enough to put yourself out there as your authentic self? And even further, do you have the courage to do it? Because let's face it: Putting yourself out there is scary. When we put ourselves out there, we are opening up to criticism and naysayers and putting ourselves at risk of getting hurt and hearing people say hurtful things. And hearing what your haters have to say on the internet? OOOUCH, not my form of enjoyment. I would much rather be at home under the covers with my Earl Grey tea latte, thank you! Nothing but cozy vibes over here. But at the end of the day, what I have come to learn is that hiding is not helping.

And the person who taught me that lesson was my mentee.

Don't Hide Yourself

My mentee and I sat down to talk about life. You know, the catch-up sessions we live for with coffee and pastries in hand. She had come to visit me, and we were going to spend a few days together. I wanted to make sure I put in the effort to support her and give the time needed to get her a clear goal for her future.

We started talking about her work and what she was doing with her social media. She loved the idea of becoming something bigger for other people to lean on in tough times and to get advice from. She had a large community in the fashion world and wanted to monetize it into something big. As we talked through some ideas of what she could do, she stared out the window and took a deep breath. Looking straight into my eyes, she said, "If I am being honest, the real thing that is holding me back isn't anything we have discussed. It's actually the fact that I don't believe I have much to offer."

We just took a moment for those words to sit in the silence and then for us to grab hold of their depth. We knew something had just been said that couldn't be taken back. It was as if saying it out loud started to take the weight off her shoulders. That belief was no longer hers to carry.

I asked why. She continued to express to me that growing up, she lived in scarcity. That they never had food on the table and always struggled to make ends meet, that this lifestyle and situation continued throughout her childhood and into her adult life. She never knew that she had an option to live differently. But most importantly, no one ever taught her how to. There wasn't a counselor, parental figure, or mentor who sat down and told her things could be different. That she could live a wealthy and abundant life. That she didn't have to struggle with money or her finances because she could create a beautiful life ahead of her.

We quickly realized that the fear holding her back was truly her mindset. Throughout this conversation, I saw so much of myself in her. I saw the same girl who believed something terrible about herself, when indeed it wasn't true. It might have been when she was younger, or when someone told her she didn't deserve it. But now, it was no longer hers to believe.

She had a choice: She could continue down this path, or she could take the steps necessary to move forward in a new direction. When we allow ourselves to be real and look our greatest fear in the eye, we diminish its power. We can look at it and wonder what we were so scared of in the first place. By being fully honest and vulnerable with me about what she was going through, we were able to tackle her fears and limiting beliefs head-on. If we don't know ourselves on the inside, how can we express ourselves on the outside?

Fast-forward a few months, I am so proud to see where that young woman is now. In just a short time, she opened her own online company for fashion styling and has been booked by a big-time celebrity for her work. Not only that, but she also started sharing her pain points from her past with others to help make an impact.

Your Authentic Truth

Living in your authentic truth means owning your past and healing the pain that you have carried for years. Once we have healed our own pain, then we can turn that pain into passion and help others heal their pains. It is one of the most rewarding and fulfilling things we can do as human beings on this earth, and I hope everyone gets to this point in their life.

The greatest gift we can give someone else is helping them see their truth. Remember, hiding your truth and who you are is not helping the very person who needs you the most: YOU. It comes full circle in every aspect of your life and soul's journey. It's yours to fully embrace and carry with you in its most healed and fulfilled form: your full, authentic, real self. If you are not on social media and you shy away from public speaking or connecting at events, you are holding back from the very community that needs you the most. If you allow the fear of rejection or failure to stop you from going to that event, then you are depriving those people who desperately need to hear your message.

Now you might be thinking, *Alexis, how do I do that? Do I just post a TikTok announcing to everyone that I'm here; it's me?*

Although I wish the algorithm were that easy, sharing who you are in order to help the community you want to reach takes practice. Let's be real: Have you ever been at dinner and gotten so bored with the conversation your mind started to wander? Or been in class as a student and wished you were anywhere but inside the classroom? I know this feeling all too well, as I'm sure you also do. It's the feeling that emerges when we don't care about the conversation happening in front of us, when the teacher or the person is sharing a story, but it doesn't really capture our attention. Instead, it makes us want to daydream about floating on clouds or think about our to-do list.

Yes, totally guilty on both counts. But what if I told you that I've learned the art of mastering how to capture someone's attention? Or at the very least, get them to stop what they are doing and listen for a few minutes. Well, the power to harness someone's attention actually begins within you, and the keys to unlocking that power are how well you know yourself and having a hype squad by your side. Yes, you read that correctly. Let me explain . . .

I was at a conference in Denver, Colorado, sitting on stage next to three other panelists. From the moment we sat down, I noticed that we had an extremely attentive audience. Women from all over the country had flown in for this conference and were eager to learn from the women on these stages. A microphone was passed down the couch from panelist to panelist to answer their subset of questions. As the first two women spoke, I took in what they were saying. As I gazed into the crowd, I noticed the energy in the room start to fade. As the panelists kept talking, I noticed that they weren't clearly answering the question. They started to get nervous and veer off into rants that had nothing to do with the actual conversation happening. The audience got more and more distracted, they weren't paying attention, half of them were on their phones, and many of them were getting up to leave.

Then it dawned on me. It doesn't matter what job you have or position you hold. If you aren't communicating yourself, your story, and your company's story effectively, then you won't reach the crowd, no matter how good or bad or prepared of a speaker you are. The women on stage at that conference could not capture the crowd's attention because they didn't see themselves or their story the way the crowd wished they would have expressed it.

You must know yourself internally in order to be brave enough to share yourself externally with the world. This goes for not only your company's brand but your personal brand as well. If we are scared and holding back, we aren't going to come across as strong leaders. Instead, we will be only half the best version of ourselves, and trust me when I say people can sense it. People know when you are holding back and not being yourself.

It's human nature to believe that if we are vulnerable about our insecurities, losses, and failures, it will make ourselves seem weak and unworthy of sharing our story. But sharing these moments about ourselves is what builds credibility as leaders. Sharing these things about ourselves allows for people to connect with us and see us for who we are. Public speaking or speaking in front of a group builds confidence in ways that repeatedly doing things doesn't. If you don't prepare, you won't be confident in your message because chances are, freestyling won't work, and people will be able to see through it.

As I waited for my turn to take the microphone, it also hit me like a ton of bricks that no one in the audience knew how nervous I was or what I was feeling. The only thing they knew was that I was on stage about to grab a microphone and talk to them. I realized quickly that the second-best gift I was given in that moment was that it didn't matter what I was thinking. It didn't matter that I was furiously thinking what my voice would sound like, what if I messed up the words, and what if I didn't say the right thing. The truth was none of that mattered. The only thing that mattered was the message.

When it was my turn, I paused and looked out into the crowd, blinded by the bright lights and the darkness of the room. I could see only the faces in the front row. Taking in a deep breath, I thought about what it would feel like to be sitting in those seats, about what those individuals sitting in the front row wanted to hear. And I realized that to truly resonate, I would have to put my fears aside and talk to the front row as easily as I would if we were sitting across from each other at dinner, and that thought put my nerves at ease.

As I began speaking and heard my voice over the loudspeakers, I stared into the eyes of the front row. They didn't care that I was sweaty or nervous; the only thing that mattered was my story and the energy of the message I was putting out into the room. My story and the ability to inspire and motivate the front row were the only things that mattered. And the fact that I had the power to inspire someone else sitting across from me was a gift and a privilege I was not going to let go to waste, not for a moment. I felt my energy shift, and I felt my connection to the audience grow stronger. They could feel what I was saying, and they gave me that energy right back.

Your Brand Needs a Hype Squad

Are you on social media? I'm sure you probably are. Do you feel like you are totally killing it—posting every day, showing up authentically, connecting with followers, and truly getting your point and messaging across correctly? I'm going to assume that it's likely you do not. And that's the thing. We might think that we're great at what we do, but if we don't express ourselves and our brand out in the world, then how will people know who we are? How will people connect with us? How will people hear about us, be inspired by us, or want to partner with us?

We need to be out there on social media, showing who we are and what we do. Sometimes we, as women, are our own worst marketers. We don't know how to showcase to the world who we are or what we do. We have to focus on our brand and how we want the world to see us. So let me ask you:

- Who are YOU?
- What do YOU stand for?
- What does your BRAND stand for?
- What's one word you want others to think when they see you?
- What emotion do you want other people to feel?
- What are the things that bring you the most joy?

So many times, we don't see ourselves the way others see us. We are hypercritical of our every move, thought, and action. And some days, we can hyperfixate on that one stupid thing we did or said that no one will remember. We don't talk about ourselves like we talk about our friends. When someone mentions my best friends or they get brought up in conversation, I can't help but jump out of my seat and gush. It's the rushing feeling of girlhood and pride overcoming me all at once. "I love her, OMG. Did you know she just got a dog and is launching her new product line and possibly moving to Paris? I've known her since I was little, and let me tell you, she's the best." Chances are, when someone asks you who your best friends are, you also jump out of your seat and start talking about them with uncontrollable excitement.

A few weeks ago, I went to breakfast with one of my best friends. I met Gigi in college, and ever since we connected in our apartment building, it was game over. Since then, no matter how many miles away we are, we pick up the phone and it's as if no time or space has passed. We have bonded over many late-night dinners of pasta, our shared sense of humor, and of course the love of our dogs.

As we walked into the restaurant, we telepathically agreed to share the blueberry pancakes and get double shot cappuccinos, a classic bestie order. We caught up about work, life, and all the above. She mentioned that she noticed I was relaunching my social media, and almost instantly, I felt my stomach drop into a bottomless pit. Being online has always been a sore spot for me, and sharing my personal life on social media has never felt comfortable or natural. In fact, it's always felt quite scary. Putting my life out there for criticism and negative comments wasn't a part of my plan.

But the conversation continued. I tried my best to explain that I was going to start posting on social media, but only for professional work and projects. It was my way of sharing, without having to share too much about my life. But as I was reeling and trying to explain myself, I knew that something was off.

Gigi told me very directly, "Alexis, how are you going to

grow a following or connect with people if you aren't sharing more about yourself?"

I hesitantly replied, "Well . . . I'm not sure. But I just know that I don't want to share too much. To be honest, I'm terrified. Sharing my personal life online?" I shook my head and buried my face in my hands.

The words that came out of Gigi's mouth next stuck with me. "Well sure, Alexis. You can continue sharing your professional life. But who wouldn't want to get to know you personally? You are a RAY of sunshine and bring so much happiness and light to everyone around you. Who wouldn't benefit from getting to know that side of you?"

Gigi has always been wise. She knew me—truly, deeply knew me—and in those moments, she saw me in a light I didn't see myself. She hyped me up and let me know it was okay to share that hype with the world.

Think about it: How often are you naturally inclined to hype yourself up on social media and share all the amazing job positions, experiences, and achievements you've ever accomplished? It's rare. Why? Because, as discussed in prior chapters, we were taught to be humble, kind, and nice, and that being boastful and audacious and loud was bad.

When I started posting on social media and doing public speaking, I used to hold myself back quite a bit. I was scared that if I said the wrong thing, I would be unfollowed or booed off the stage and asked to never return. I would come home and tear myself into a million pieces. I was the conductor of the self-hate train, and there was nothing that could stop me on those tracks. Except for my friends. I remember going to lunch with two of my closest girlfriends and telling them about this feeling. When I said it out loud, they both immediately looked at me and replied, "Are you crazy?" They were not only my reality check in that moment, but they were also the support I needed to get back up and keep going.

One of the most important things on your journey to self-expression is your hype squad. My hype squad is made up of a variety of different women—best friends from high school, colleagues, and work friends. These women represent what girlhood is about. They have pulled me out of the depths of my fears that would have stopped me from going for it. Fear never fully disappears. We all have that little voice in our heads that will continue to make us feel queasy right before something big happens. But that voice and those fears are natural, so give yourself some grace and keep moving forward. What got me to stand on stages and authentically connect and engage with my audience was learning how my friends saw me through their perspective. It wasn't until I heard the feedback from my friends that I started to see my story and my experiences differently.

Here is my solution for you: Pick three women to be your very own hype squad. These are going to be the friends who will hold up a mirror to you and say, "This is how you think you are being perceived, and this is how you are actually showing up." Most of the time, those perceptions are different, and you deserve to know how your friends and the world truly see you. I want you to ask them all tonight to hype you up, and by that, I mean I want you to ask them to share the things they value and see in you as strengths that go far beyond the rest.

Here's the key: I want you to listen closely, and when they say something that makes you think, *Wait, really?*, remember it because that, my friends, is what I want you to share with the world. These are the things—those special qualities, stories, and parts of you that your truest and closest friends in your hype squad can see—that sometimes you don't see in yourself. These are the things we need to get comfortable sharing on stages, on social, and within our communities, no matter how scary or strange to you they might sound at first. Trust that your squad has your back and that they will be there for you to keep showing up for yourself, even on those days when it doesn't feel like you can do it.

I give you all permission to bring your full self to the table. Today, I want you to show up on social media and showcase to the world your brand. Trust me, the world needs you, and if you are Latina, we need your background showcased now more than ever before. When I show up, sometimes I speak Spanglish; sometimes I don't. Sometimes I decide to go blonde; sometimes I'm brunette. Some days I feel like eating Cuban food, others Chinese food. But those are all aspects of my true self and my version of what it means to be Cuban, and that should be shared because there are a community and group of people who will resonate with that. Your story, your background, your heritage, and your experiences—all those things that make up who you are—are the things that people in this world are waiting to know and learn and LOVE about you.

So just remember, you cannot attract an authentic audience if you aren't putting yourself out there. The world needs you to show up as you are. The hardest part is being brave enough to do it.

CHAPTER 11

TAKING CENTER STAGE

I've loved being on stages since I can remember: countless hours of practicing while pacing my bathroom floor and the feeling of jitters right before the lights go on. Exhilaration and fear all roll into one emotion at the pit of my stomach. But in the end, I wouldn't change a thing. Because after every recital, speech, or presentation, the result is the same: connecting with people and deep fulfillment. And those early recitals turned into giving graduation speeches and ultimately to speaking on large corporate stages in front of hundreds of people. Those corporate stages led me to conferences, both as an attendee and as a speaker.

Conferences have taught me about different types of industries, businesses, sales methods, leadership techniques, and everything in between. I have learned how to give constructive feedback and how to be a supportive fan. I have learned to cheer people on after they finish a big speech. I have learned how to communicate my gratitude to speakers and group members and how to really soak up the words that people are saying and feel their wins and losses. I have learned how to network. I have learned to appreciate how special it is for someone to share their story with you and how we should relish in those moments of being in an audience. I have learned how to speak to others in awkward settings and bounce back after someone says a joke that didn't land (and how to be that person's friend by reminding them that no one will remember). I have learned how to listen to others' stories. I have learned how to take notes and come back to them a few weeks later to implement the best parts.

Ultimately, each conference I have attended has filled my cup: the ones I've spoken at, the ones I've participated in, and the ones I've attended as an audience member. Every moment on stage, every interaction off stage, every keynote and panel discussion I've led, and every debrief with audience members. I look back on every conference and smile.

Taking the Mic

Imagine the moment right before the curtain on a stage goes up. It's a pivotal moment, a moment that makes you feel queasy but exhilarated all at the same time. You've been practicing, you know you are ready, and you deserve it. It's the moment of truth. While waiting backstage, you hear the emcee's footsteps behind you. They tap you on the shoulder, and you hear them whisper, "You're next," as they walk onto the stage. They introduce you, and as they say their last words, the crowd falls silent. You see the lights dim and the curtain go up. The director looks at you, points, and says, "Go, NOW!"

It's your moment. You walk onto the stage, grab the microphone, and pause. As you gaze across the room, you know you have the crowd's undivided attention. No one is on their phone. They are all looking at you. There are no distractions; it's just you and your voice sounding through the speakers. The audience is listening to what you have to say. Truly listening, not the listening where they are just thinking about what to say in response, but the type of listening where they are hearing a person's full story and perspective from their point of view. Microphones and the people holding them on stage have power. They command an audience's respect, attention, and silence.

The power of a microphone is one that every woman deserves. To go out there and be heard. To go out there and share yourself. It's a vulnerable moment. But it's also the most rewarding. Why? Because you not only prove to yourself you can do it but you also deliver a message that impacts those you are presenting to. The reward is in knowing that your performance can leave a mark on someone. My wish for every woman is to embrace their voice and find their stage, whether it's a big stage or a small stage, a large national platform or your local city council, a national conference or your company's marketing department. Your stage can be whatever and wherever you want it to be. But I urge all of you to find your spotlight.

Now, hold on a second because I can see all my introverts slowly slinking away from that paragraph. I do not want anyone who has stage fright or who is an introvert to feel like this doesn't apply to them, because it does. Finding your stage doesn't have to be with hundreds of lights and people staring at you. It can be as simple as running your own business meetings. I want you to create whatever stage is most comfortable for you, big or small. "Being on your stage" simply means being heard as your authentic self.

So no excuses, introverts! I want all of you to treat your small groups and town hall meetings as your very own opportunity to have the stage. Find and command the attention in a room, whichever room you choose, and bring it. Bring your talent, passion, and voice, and have your authenticity move through the speakers and vibrate throughout the room. It's about being heard and seen. It's about sharing your message and being listened to by a group of people. Because what truly matters are connection and collaboration. Give yourself permission to command authority and power in a room. Get comfortable with it. Be heard, be seen, and be loved for your authentic self.

Society has held women back for many years, and as a result, society has impacted the way we see and believe in ourselves. We have held ourselves back from expressing how we really feel, being bold, and sharing our talents with the world. But not anymore. Now is our time, and your stage is waiting for you. The question is, are you ready?

Imagine yourself walking onto your new stage, or maybe you are walking down the halls of Congress for your first hearing as an elected official. Maybe you are walking to your first meeting as a CEO or walking into a classroom to give a presentation to students. Maybe you are walking onto the stage of your first Broadway play or into your first art gallery showing. Maybe you are walking to your first TED Talk. Maybe you are walking to your first time on the trading floor in New York City. Know that as we each walk onto our stage, we are not only empowering the women around us but we are also paving thc way for the next generation coming behind us. Each time we walk onto a stage that lacks representation, we are making our voices heard and impacting everyone around us.

What will your stage be, and what will it give to you in return? Will it bring you great joy and excitement? Will you feel lit up inside and flowing with buckets of energy? Will you feel at peace knowing your work is fulfilling? Think about who will be there with you. Consider what your greatest hope for your work is and how you can best share that hope. Ask yourself what unleashing your authenticity and sharing yourself with others will feel like, what standing there on your stage will be like. Then bring it into existence. Find your stage.

Conferences gave me the ultimate gift: the gift of knowing

that my power comes from connecting with others, knowing that accomplishing something on my own is meaningless, and knowing that getting together with large groups of people for a bigger purpose serves me and fulfills me. I've also learned that it can be rewarding to put yourself out there and share your story with others because, chances are, everyone in the room can relate to you on a different level. The value isn't in me or my perfect speaking abilities; it's in the message and the story that are being delivered. I am forever grateful for conferences because they gave me the gift of my voice. They allowed me to embrace myself to my fullest and go for it, to leave it all on the floor and not hold back, and to give it my all and allow for inspiration to occur.

Taking Up Space

"What if you become a professional and motivational speaker?" my friend asked curiously. "You're always talking about conferences, you love them, and you light up whenever you get the chance to share. So why not just create your own conference?"

Simple and to the point. A question that hadn't really crossed my mind before. But after I heard it, I couldn't get it out of my head. For weeks after my friend said those words to me, they echoed in my head. I had so many unanswered thoughts, questions I didn't have answers for, and ideas that were incomplete. How was I going to get people to come?

What if we couldn't find the right location? What if no one showed up and it was just me and a table of food? *Was I even good enough to do this?*

Wait. Just. A. Moment. Please hold. What?

That last sentence stopped me in my tracks. *Nope*, I thought. *Not today, and definitely not this one.* For the first time, when I said those words, I knew the answer. Not even my endless loop of self-doubt could stop me from living out this idea. Something deep inside of me knew I had to do this. No matter if it was just me and a few people. Because realistically, I would rather try than not try at all. I knew that this, specifically speaking and conferences, was worth giving a shot and betting on myself. Because if there was anyone who could do it, give it their all, and still enjoy it no matter the outcome, it would be me.

I gave it more thought and started to work through the details. There is no greater gift than sharing your passions with the world. And to be able to create my own talk? Created by women, for women. I have never felt more in my own element than knowing my work is bringing together women for a higher cause. And the best part? If I could cater to a female audience, then I could inspire and teach women who wanted to find their own stages.

What was I waiting for?

What are WE waiting for?

When I started to put together the elements, I knew I

wanted to create a magical experience, one that brought together brilliant and inspiring minds to share their stories with other women seeking mentorship and role models in their lives, women wanting to feel reignited and reenergized to come alive on their own stages. I wanted to inspire other women to take that next leap and do the things they'd been wanting to do for a while, all while being able to connect with a new community of women. I wanted these women to build relationships and learn insights on how others got to where they are and how they could get there themselves.

What I wanted to create was the ideal talk I wish I had heard ten years ago, one that would bring together all the elements of my own journey and struggles, but one that also motivated, inspired, and built community. I wanted them to leave and have the confidence to network with incredible leaders today, find mentors and people they wanted to be, and obtain the support to get there.

I wanted women to sit down and talk about what is really holding them back and what it is they truly believe about themselves. I wanted inspiration to come from all sides, angles, and perspectives. It is through community that we can find what brings out the light inside of us. What inspires one person won't inspire another. We are all different, which is why it's so important to bring a variety of industries, backgrounds, ethnicities, and people together.

I also knew we had to create something to support young

female small business owners who lacked capital. We all know the obstacles that come with raising venture capital. We all know the facts: Only 2% of all venture capital funding goes to women,[1] which is one of the most frustrating parts of being a female business leader. You can have an amazing idea, but without funding or proof of insane sales, your business may not grow.

Then it hit me: Why not combine the conference with a grant program? I started to research how I could provide grants or monetary support for small business owners. And just like that our Small Business Grant for Las Vegas Entrepreneurs was created. In the fall of 2025, we would offer a $10,000 grant for female-run small businesses that had been in business for a year.

By the time this book comes out, the conference will have already happened. The days and nights spent planning the details and bringing all the creativity to life will all have been worth it. And truthfully, working on a project like this was the greatest joy of my life. My vision for The Business of Her Conference was to create an event and community that deeply wanted more for themselves. We invited industry leaders from all types of businesses to speak on their experiences, candidly and authentically, on stage. We even reached out to a doctor of psychology who focuses on removing career blocks for women through a data lens. When I tell you I couldn't be more excited for this conference, I really mean it. It was created for the next generation of women to take up space and become the leaders they were destined to be.

Every detail from the brand colors to breakout sessions to a Pinot and Prosecco Happy Hour was created from my heart for yours. The truth about connecting in real time is this: So often as women, we focus on everything else—kids, carpool calendars, marriage, household, you name it. But this day is for women to take time for themselves, to turn inward, self-reflect, realign, and then grow outwardly and rise to lead.

I want those women to walk away and finally *get on stage*. I want women to take the stage in business, in government, in health care, and in philanthropy—whatever that stage is for them. I want for others exactly what I wanted for myself: to be bold enough and have the courage to get up on that stage and speak the words you want others to hear. "See you on stage" is quite literally my wish for women. It's representative of where I want to see women because I want them to be heard, respected, comfortable, and confident in their own skin to speak their truth.

But to get on stage, we must believe in ourselves and have confidence to get up there. It takes courage to put yourself out there. It takes practice and a personal review of your beliefs. Do you believe you deserve to be heard? Do you believe you are worthy of all good things in life? Love, family, financial security, and anything you desire are there for you, but you have to believe you are worthy of them. You have to believe you deserve them.

CHAPTER 12

IT'S SHOWTIME

When's the last time you read a book that you couldn't put down? A book that was so captivating and consuming you couldn't get up off your couch because you had to know what happens next. Can you think of one?

It's been a while since I've read a book like that. Maybe it's the fact that we are all glued to our phones nowadays. Or maybe it's because my attention span has admittedly been cut short to last about thirty seconds. Even with my latest attempts of hours spent at Barnes & Noble lurking down the aisles and spending more money at the checkout counter than I planned, I find it difficult to pinpoint the last time my imagination wandered. It's like the books have become so predictable that it's not worth reading the rest of the chapters.

When I gave it some thought, I realized the last book I couldn't put down was Nicole Walters's book *Nothing Is Missing*. From the moment I opened the book, I couldn't get enough. She was captivating in a relatable way and never strayed from being real and honest, sharing the highs and lows of her life without reservation. Reading it was intoxicating, and when I got to the last page, I was sad it was over. That's how you really know you loved a book.

When I think about other books that had a similar effect on me, the one thing they had in common was that they were stories about women, either autobiographies or self-help that shared the author's personal stories at some point throughout the book. You're probably wondering why I find myself in this pattern, as was I. After giving it some thought, and many failed fiction purchases later, what I have learned is that many fiction books are predictable. You can most likely guess the ending, or variations of the ending, and probably be 80 percent correct.

But the thing about reading self-help and nonfiction stories is that the endings are unpredictable. And not only are the endings unpredictable, but so is everything in between: the twenty times they fell before they achieved their goals, the icky feelings of pain and conflict they felt before getting into their dream relationship, or the rejections and criticisms they faced while building something for themselves. No one actually knows what happens in a person's life. And that's exactly why I can't put these books down. Because I need to know how she did it, how she moved through that conflict, overcame her insecurities, and dealt with the pain of rejection and stinging criticism.

That is what I want to know about. Why? Because I feel it too. I know those feelings deeply and can honestly relate. And when I can relate and understand someone's story, I can apply it to my life and grow. Well, that is the true source of magic. I am obsessed with learning from other women's stories about their lives because that's where the change happens. I am certain of it.

I will admit I am new to being an author. At times, the thought of putting my work out into the world was a bit scary. But the more I wrote, the better I got. And a secret that helped me even more? Reading books—as many as possible. The more books I read, the better I became at understanding how to write and put myself in the shoes of the reader. I became obsessed with reading, not only for learning how to write, but also learning about women's stories. My shelves started to fill up with different colored spines stacked against each other. Some of my favorite books are memoirs, as we rarely get to know someone fully. For me, memoirs feel like a one-on-one session with a person and their entire life.

I became obsessed with every woman's story—how they overcame their fears, how they started their companies, how they juggled careers and families, and so on. I realized that every story was unique and that each woman had to go through ups and downs to get to where she is. But the one thing they all had in common was that they kept going.

As I continued to read these stories, something struck a chord with me. I wasn't the only one obsessed with learning from other women. Girls are no longer looking to the beautiful celebrities and Disney princesses; they are looking to female CEOs and leaders. Talk about a huge societal shift. Our media is showcasing and highlighting incredible female leaders. Our media is portraying women in roles that were usually filled by men. Hello Sunshine, an initiative from Reese Witherspoon, has brought an entirely new spin to how books, shows, and movies are made—the female way. This shift is a cultural one that I couldn't be happier to see and be a part of.

CEOs Are the New Cinderellas

The more women who create and bring their ideas into the world, the more spotlights we have to shine on them, and the more the next wave of girls will aspire to do the same.

It's a new era. Women are rising and leading in ways we haven't before. We are continuing to break down and push boundaries that have been in place for years. We are becoming leaders and advocates across the globe. We are leading organizations and countries. We are growing our companies and organizations at a rapid pace. We are at a point in our nation's history where we are leading stronger and more powerfully than we ever have before. But as we continue to move forward, we must remember that all of this is only possible because of the people who came before us.

Let's thank the women who came before us and made our current realities possible. Thank you to the women who got us the right to vote, the right to a bank account, and the right to work. Thank you to the women in the '90s who started their own businesses and became role models for us today. Thank you, Sheryl Sandberg and Melinda French Gates, for paving the way forward for women's rights and our ability to be seen and recognized as real leaders regardless of our gender.

But as we pave the way forward for the women who will come behind us, what is it you want to see improved? There's still great inequality in the workplace with the income gap and gender biases. Minority women aren't being advocated for in boardrooms and get passed up because of their race. There are moms about to get pregnant with their next child whose business venture won't get accepted or funded because of their next family member.

In a world today where women's rights are being taken away, it feels as if we are going back in time. With certain leaders de-prioritizing our health, well-being, funding, and overall support, it can feel disappointing and disheartening. It can feel impossible to overcome or to get back to where we were, but that is exactly why we can't sit on the sidelines. We can't allow others to take our power. So many times, we think that we are small, and what is our one voice even worth? But it is enough. Our voice is more than enough, and it is so desperately needed. Every person and every woman counts in this.

But what will you be responsible for? Will you hire an all-female team? Will you teach and lead a class for men to educate them on biases? Will you invest your money in female entrepreneurs as an angel investor? Will you mentor the next female mayor in your area? How will you help the next generation of women?

Everyone has a story to tell and a part to play in this movement. Collectively, we each contribute to the way our societal structures are set. If we each do our own part, then our change will be bigger. But doing your own part can be as simple as living out your calling, living your truth, living authentically to you and your purpose, and being that example for others to see. That is enough. That is more than enough. You are owning your voice and power, commanding respect and giving respect, and showing that your gender does not define you. Your heart, contributions, and talents are what matter. Set boundaries for others to see you for your merit and hard work, not for your gender. Live your values in alignment with being you.

Your story is yours and no one else's. There will be big wins, incredible aha moments, and pockets of pure joy. But there will also be grief, moments of sadness, and epic failures that will make your stomach flip inside out and make you wonder why you tried at all.

But it's the unique tie that brings all our stories together, that each of us will have our own set of failures and lessons, wins and losses to share. So don't feel ashamed, please! Because guess what? The person next to you in the doctor's waiting room or on an airplane has also experienced great joy and has also failed. There's something to learn from everyone, and each of our stories deserves to be told. It took my entire journey of ups and downs to get to where I am now. It took the failures, the lessons, and the heartbreaks. It took practice, time, and grace for myself. It took friends, family, and support systems. It took a strong belief in myself that at some point in time I would figure out what my passion was and go for it. It's been a journey of self-discovery. One where I've come to love and accept myself.

I've come to find that nothing is more rewarding than doing something you believe in. When it comes from within, like a burning message inside of you that you have to get out, I promise there's a reason for it. Most likely, it's your body's way of telling you to express it. Share your thoughts, gifts, talents, and creativity with the world. Whatever it is, go for it. The scariest and hardest part is starting. Planning conferences, convening people, and impacting women have never made me happier. Although it seems scary when we are starting something new, we just have to start. We might make mistakes along the way, but our momentum is moving.

Take the time to figure out what it is for you. What

message do you want to share with the world? Because only you can deliver it in your own special and unique way. The world is waiting for you to share your message. It's time.

As you prepare and rehearse for your stage, remember to always turn inward. Know that the answers you want are within you, even though you may have the urge to turn to others. Remember to create your support bench and turn to it whenever you need a gentle reminder that you and everything you do matter. Continue building your group of mentors and role models for guidance and inspiration. They will help you expand your horizons and continue to grow beyond your expectations.

As they continue to grow in strength and number, women will continue to find and own their power. They will bring their highest and greatest projects, aspirations, and dreams into fruition for the benefit of our society collectively. And as this group continues to surface and build, it will create new societal beliefs. Collectively, we will change the narrative. We will build new belief systems and realities for our gender. Increasing our power as leaders will allow for parity across industries. It will allow for new laws and structures to be built that are fair and just. It will allow for women to receive equity in society and stand on their own.

When I look back at the hardships and tough moments I've experienced, I now understand that they all happened for a reason. It's hard to believe, but I know it to be true. Every time I give mentorship guidance to a young woman, I know exactly what NOT to do. Why? Because I will never allow another woman to experience what I did.

Looking back, I am grateful for those moments because they made me the mentor, leader, and businesswoman I am today. They shaped my values and allowed me to create my own rules on how to mentor young women and create events. Being told I was never going to succeed and my event would be an embarrassment taught me to never shut down a mentee's idea. It taught me that my job is not to criticize their ideas; it is my job to help support and grow their ideas, no matter how good or bad they might be.

Because the truth is, if that little voice inside of them is shouting "Start that chocolate business" or "Run for office," it is not my job to tear them down and tell them how hard it is going to be. Instead, it is my job to provide them with solutions on how to move forward and make that dream or idea a reality. Because at the end of the day, the only one who will regret not starting that business or running for office is them. And if they never try because they are too scared or I told them not to, twenty years from now, they will look back, always wonder "what if," and regret never trying. I would rather help my mentees try and then fail than never try at all. Because even if they do fail, there was so much they learned along the way. And those experiences and skills add to their life résumé, which is never a waste of time. In the moment, when I got torn down, it was easy to be angry and upset. But looking back, I am so grateful for those moments because they helped me become an incredible mentor and advocate for young women.

The passion to advocate for women is strong inside me, one that will never cease. It's a fire I will carry with me for a lifetime. A fire that burns so deeply it cannot be silenced or blown out. It's forever burning. Speaking on stages is a gift because speaking for hundreds of young women allows for impact and change to happen. And that is something I can't and won't take lightly because deep down, when I was in the audience or in their seats as a young woman, I knew that feeling of not belonging, of being less than.

This collective power is the energy and community I want to bring together. Over the next twenty years, great things will change for women. I want to highlight those of us brave enough to be a part of the change. I hope to highlight these incredible achievements and movements happening across the nation. I want to capture these moments, year after year, as a collection of moments in history that mark our microchanges that ultimately will lead to parity and close the gender gap.

The stage is set for us. The lights have never been brighter. They're our female stories to tell, and we are just getting started. So turn up the volume, turn it all the way up. Get ready to be heard, be seen, and live authentically yourself.

So, come one and come all to the magical show where brilliant female minds come alive across the nation, each in her own city, state, workplace, and community. Clicking on their microphones, one by one. Together over time, collectively creating community. As your emcee on her own stage, I promise to use my powers and resources to make progress. With each conference, each speaking engagement, and each talk that I give, I will be an advocate. I promise to encourage and bring together women from across the nation to share their stories on stages, to inspire each other, to support one another on the journey of self-discovery, and to cheer you on the journey of making your dreams a reality.

If you have a passion. If you have a product. If you have an idea. If you're a future leader. If you're a future artist. If you're a future creative. If you're a future ambassador. If you're a future teacher. If you're a future governor. If you're a future mentor. If you want to share your story, I welcome you all.

Come and join us. Hear me when I say that I want to be your biggest advocate. I want to share your story, your passion, and your product. I want you to be part of this female community of creative thinkers who push the limits. I want to share the light and give you the stage. So, take the stage. The world can't wait to hear your story, and I can't wait to help you share it.

CHAPTER 13

MY LOVE LETTER TO YOU

I decided that this book wouldn't be complete without a love letter written to all the women reading it. I wanted to let you know that although you may be just starting your self-discovery journey or in the process of refining it, we are all works in progress, at every age and at every stage, including myself. I'll be the first to admit that I've made so many mistakes and said and done things I wish I hadn't. But everyone does, and we must forgive ourselves, move forward, and see it as a learning opportunity. There are always ways to improve and make ourselves better.

Dear Women,
If no one has said this to you today or this year, let me be the one to tell you:

I believe in you.

I believe that you have the power, abilities, talents, and

gifts that are needed in this world. I know deep down that you belong, that your voice matters, that you bring something amazing to the table. You can accomplish your goals and remove your self-limiting beliefs over time with awareness and practice. You can get up every day and have a deep and strong belief in yourself and your abilities. You can practice your strength every day and become fully confident in your abilities. You can be a leader in this world, and you can create something amazing.

Right now, in this very moment, I want all of you to take the time to really appreciate yourselves. Give yourself grace and gratitude for everything you have been through and conquered and be excited for all the good things to come.

You are extraordinary—for all the beauty you hold within you, for the love you have in your heart, for the goodness you hold within for others around you, and for the hope you have for a better world to live in. You are so loved. Even when others make you feel otherwise. Know that although things may feel painful at times, moving through it will bring you a greater and stronger relationship with yourself than you ever knew was possible. I'm saddened by all the pain that you've gone through and suffered, for others making you feel small, less than, and unworthy.

But you, my dear, are none of those things. Your power lies within knowing and believing the truth. It may take you some time, years, friends, and life experiences to realize and find it.

But I promise that once you get there, you'll look back and be so grateful it all ended up that way. You will be grateful for all the good and bad that happened. Your power lies in recognizing and seeing yourself as the magnetic, loving, genuine, happy soul that you are. And that is where your passion is ignited. Turning pain into passion for a lifetime is well worth the journey, leading to the moment you can look in the mirror and see you for you, not for what others have made you believe you are.

You just need to believe in YOU. Remember, if you gave something your all and it didn't work out, it wasn't meant to be for you, and the setback will make you stronger. Everyone has a story worth telling and being heard. You must have the courage and the confidence to share it. Your voice is valuable and impactful. You are strong. You deserve to know your worth and to stand back up when things don't go your way. Fight for whatever it is that you believe in. And if something makes you angry, remember it is just your body's way of telling you something; listen to it. Stay true to you and always stay kind because karma will reward you for how you act and what you do. For those who have wronged you, remember that justice and karma will always find a way to the surface. Don't be discouraged by setbacks or failures, because they will ultimately end up being your greatest teachers and motivators in life.

You are worth all the blessings, joy, and love this world has to offer. Make sure to travel often and bring those you love with you. Your experiences will shape you, and the people around you will both support you and challenge you. Know that there are good men in this world, and I believe we can work with them, be in loving relationships with them, and raise them. Not all of them will see our power, but know that the ones that will are there for us 100 percent of the way.

Don't let anyone dim your light. No matter what someone says or does, know that you have the power to block them from interfering with your beliefs. Whatever you feel called to do in this life, don't doubt it for a second. Those feelings are there for a reason, and you deserve to honor them. The only person you will disappoint in trying something is yourself. The biggest regret most people discover in their old age is living a life for someone else. Live the life YOU desire—that is your soul's deepest desire and one of the most fulfilling things you can do.

Your soul is ready to be heard and for you to listen. Your soul and heart will never misguide you. They will lead you to answers and lessons about yourself that will allow you to understand yourself and the world in new ways. And taking time to listen from within will only improve your life for the better. Your gut and intuition are the strongest guides to your life. They are your internal compass to life. You just need to be ready to listen. When it all gets quiet and you find yourself ready, you can take that deep dive within. You can truly listen without judgment or hesitation. You can allow for subconscious thoughts and desires to emerge. The time you spend on yourself is an investment you'll never regret.

Pour your heart into every aspect of your life and do not look back. Be a light to someone every day and call that a success. Show love and compassion to your coworkers, friends, and community, and believe in your soul that working in diverse teams brings the best results for the people and world around us. Know that this is my wish for all of you moving forward. I believe in you. There is nothing you can't do, only things that you don't want to do. So, what is it you are about to begin? Because the world is waiting and wants to know.

You are ready. Even though you might think you're not or feel the fear of failure looming, let me be the first to tell you to just start. Even through the fear, you can begin slowly. And every time you try, you will prove to yourself that it wasn't that bad and that you can do it. You've done the work, you've put in the time, and you've spent your energy on building yourself and your beliefs. You are stronger now than you were before, and you have the tools, guidance, and support to get you there. You can turn this life into exactly what you want it to be. And you can enjoy the time you spend on the journey getting there.

I vow to do my part every day to inspire, teach, and lead the next generation of women to believe in themselves and have the confidence to wake up every day doing what they love and being authentically themselves. I don't have all the answers, but I want to be a part of the solution for change. Who's in?

It's time for all women to take their stage. One industry, one passion, and one business idea at a time. Draw the curtain and cue the lights: It's showtime.

See you on stage.

—Alexis Meruelo

ADDITIONAL RESOURCES

GETTING YOU READY FOR POWER PLAYBOOK

PHASE 1 **Believing in Yourself: Building Self-Worth and Confidence**	**PHASE 2** **Building Your Team: Role Models, Mentors, and Support Groups**	**PHASE 3** **Rising to Lead: Achieving Your Goals, Landing Your Dream Career, and Stepping into Power**
• Going Inward: Self-Discovery and Understanding	• Getting to Know Yourself • Being Your #1 Hype Woman • Sharing It with the World	• Taking Center Stage and Stepping into Your Own Light
• Releasing Old Beliefs and Rewriting Your Core Beliefs	• Asking for Mentorship • Getting the Mentor You Want • Advocating for Yourself	• Showing up and Sharing Yourself Online and in the World Authentically as YOU
• Strengths + Practice – Self-Doubt = Confidence • Self-Worth = Unconditional Love for Yourself Always • Building Your New Home Foundation	• Discovering and Building Your Purpose—Known for XYZ • Building Your Support Bench	• Leading Boldly in Rooms Where Decisions, Influence, and Impact Are Made

ACKNOWLEDGMENTS

Thank you to the numerous amazing individuals who made this book possible. First and foremost, thank you to my literary agent at Wonderwell Press, Maggie; my editors Chrissy and Melanie; Kristen; and the entire team at Greenleaf Book Group! This would not have been possible without you. Thank you for believing in me and helping me bring this book to life.

To my mother, thank you for the constant outpouring of love and support, the daily phone calls, and the genuine care you have given me. Your grace and integrity are timeless—qualities I am honored to have inherited by just being around you. You don't ever get the acknowledgments or praise you so deeply deserve, so here it is, my twin soul and life's angel, I love you.

To my sister, to know we will always be in each other's lives is a gift. Thank you for the love and support as we both continue our life journeys. Know that I'll be here to cheer you on every step of the way of living your soul's purpose.

JM—thank you for it ALL. This wouldn't have been possible without your unwavering support and conviction in my success. I can only hope people feel the same joy we do calling each other on the phone and being together. The one thing you've made clear: There's no bigger gift in life than having a best friend that feels like home.

To my girlfriends Gigi, Jenny, Mary, Meghan, Tita, Maria, and Sophia. My greatest joys have been because of you: the travels, the memories, the food, the laughs, the late-night calls, the shopping trips, the bottomless iced coffees and boba. The outpouring of love and support on the best days and wine on the late nights have and will stay with me for a lifetime. Thank you for showing me that your presence can get me through the hardest of times. And that real friendships are about loving that other person in that exact moment and life stage they are in. You've allowed me to share all parts of me and given me the gift of perspective, which allowed me to grow into the person I've become. I wouldn't trade any of it for the world—and I would travel that very world just to see you.

To my mentees, you have given me so much fulfillment in this lifetime. Thank you for believing in me to provide you the guidance, respect, and support you need on your career journeys. Watching you start to believe in yourselves is the greatest form of fulfillment my heart has endured, and I will forever be grateful for you putting your trust in me. Maria, Sarah,

Natalia, Daniella, and Brooklyn, I can't wait to see where you all go from here! The sky is the limit for you girls.

To my mentors, Nina, Melissa, Colleen, Anita, Savera, Tracey, Keith, and Cid, thank you for teaching me and showing me the way. Watching you lead at work has helped me create my own version of how I want to show up and lead in the world, for myself and for others.

And finally, I would be remiss without thanking Sadie girl. Thanks for the love and being by my side, my sweet little love.

NOTES

INTRODUCTION

1. Solomon Amar, “Why Everyone Wins with More Women in Leadership,” *Forbes*, February 7, 2023, https://www.forbes.com/councils/forbesbusinesscouncil/2023/02/07/why-everyone-wins-with-more-women-in-leadership/.
2. “Are Female CEOs Better Than Male CEOs?,” Personal Finance Club, March 7, 2023, updated March 18, 2024, https://www.personalfinanceclub.com/are-female-ceos-better-than-male-ceos/.
3. Sonali Basak and Jeff Green, “Female CFOs Brought in $1.8 Trillion More Than Male Peers,” Bloomberg Law, October 16, 2019, https://news.bloomberglaw.com/esg/female-cfos-brought-in-1-8-trillion-more-than-male-peers/.
4. Amar, “Why Everyone Wins.”

CHAPTER 1

1. Luciana Paulise, “75% of Women Executives Experience Imposter Syndrome in the Workplace,” *Forbes*, March 8, 2023, https://www.forbes.com/sites/lucianapaulise/2023/03/08/75-of-women-executives-experience-imposter-syndrome-in-the-workplace/.
2. Melinda French Gates, *The Moment of Lift: How Empowering Women Changes the World* (Flatiron Books, 2019), 222.
3. Ruchika Tulshyan and Jodi-Ann Burey, “Stop Telling Women They Have Imposter Syndrome,” *Harvard Business Review*, February 11, 2021, https://hbr.org/2021/02/stop-telling-women-they-have-imposter-syndrome.
4. Prof. Kristen Collett-Schmitt, Notre Dame Elevate Program, 2023.

5. "Underestimated Start-Up Founders: The Untapped Opportunity," McKinsey & Company, June 23, 2023, https://www.mckinsey.com/featured-insights/diversity-and-inclusion/underestimated-start-up-founders-the-untapped-opportunity/.
6. Women Business Collaborative, "8.8% Fortune 500 CEOs Are Women—the Highest of All Indices—According to the Women CEOs in America Report 2022," *PR Newswire*, September 22, 2022, https://www.prnewswire.com/news-releases/8-8-fortune-500-ceos-are-women---the-highest-of-all-indices--according-to-the-women-ceos-in-america-report-2022--301630455.html.
7. Carmen Sesin, "Latinos Are 'Vastly' Underrepresented on Corporate Boards," NBC News, September 23, 2022, https://www.nbcnews.com/news/latino/latinos-are-vastly-underrepresented-corporate-boards-rcna49022.
8. Contessa Brewer and Jessica Golden, "Latinos Are Seeing the Least Amount of Growth in Corporate Board Representation, New Findings Show," CNBC, September 23, 2022, https://www.cnbc.com/2022/09/23/over-60percent-of-fortune-1000-corporate-boards-lack-latino-representation.html.
9. Rohit Arora, "Hispanic Heritage Month: Examining Latino-Owned Business Success," *Forbes*, September 26, 2023, https://www.forbes.com/sites/rohitarora/2023/09/26/hispanic-heritage-month-examining-latino-owned-business-success/?sh=22a84729153f.
10. Pooneh Baghai, Olivia Howard, Lakshmi Prakash, and Jill Zucker, "Women as the Next Wave of Growth in US Wealth Management," McKinsey & Company, July 2020, https://www.mckinsey.com/~/media/McKinsey/Industries/Financial%20Services/Our%20Insights/Women%20as%20the%20next%20wave%20of%20growth%20in%20US%20wealth%20management/Women-as-the-next-wave-of-growth-in-US-wealth-management.pdf.

CHAPTER 2

1. Stacey Lindsay, "Jamie Kern Lima Says This Is the One Thing You Need to Change Your Life," Sunday Paper PLUS, February 24, 2024, https://www.mariashriversundaypaper.com/jamie-kern-lima-worthy/.
2. "Get the Facts: Body Image," National Organization for Women, accessed October 2, 2024, https://now.org/now-foundation/love-your-body/love-your-body-whats-it-all-about/get-the-facts/.

3. Amelia Hill, "Social Media Triggers Children to Dislike Their Own Bodies, Says Study," *The Guardian*, January 1, 2023, https://www.theguardian.com/society/2023/jan/01/social-media-triggers-children-to-dislike-their-own-bodies-says-study.

CHAPTER 3

1. Jack Canfield and Mark Victor Hansen, *The Aladdin Factor: How to Ask for What You Want—and Get It* (Berkley Books, 1995).
2. Canfield and Hansen, *Aladdin Factor*.
3. John Traugott, "Achieving Your Goals: An Evidence-Based Approach," Michigan State University Extension, August 26, 2014, https://www.canr.msu.edu/news/achieving_your_goals_an_evidence_based_approach.

CHAPTER 4

1. Eyder Peralta, "Sheryl Sandberg: The Word 'Bossy' Should Be Banned," NPR, March 9, 2014, https://www.npr.org/sections/thetwo-way/2014/03/09/288307452/sheryl-sandberg-the-word-bossy-should-be-banned/.
2. Gabrielle Bernstein, *The Universe Has Your Back: Transform Fear to Faith* (Hay House, 2016).
3. Eli Amdur, "12 Essentials to Creating a Culture of Creativity," *Forbes*, September 12, 2022, https://www.forbes.com/sites/eliamdur/2022/09/12/12-essentials-to-creating-a-culture-of-creativity/.
4. "The Confidence Collapse and Why It Matters for the Next Gen," The Confidence Code for Girls and YPulse, October 2018, https://iwlca.wordpress.com/wp-content/uploads/2018/10/f778b-theconfidencecodeforgirlsxypulse.pdf.

CHAPTER 5

1. Rodrigo Dominguez-Villegas, "COVID Increased Latinas' Responsibilities at Home While Limiting Their Ability to Work," UCLA Newsroom, September 8, 2022, https://newsroom.ucla.edu/releases/latinas-covid-home-responsibilities-and-work.

2. "Machismo," Dictionary.com, accessed April 2024, https://www.dictionary.com/browse/machismo/.
3. Hugo Quintana, "Machismo Culture Must Go," *The Michigan Daily*, March 17, 2021, https://www.michigandaily.com/michigan-in-color/machismo-culture-must-go/.
4. Misael Galdámez and Gabriella Carmona, "All Work and No Pay: Unpaid Latina Care Work During the Covid-19 Pandemic," UCLA Latino Policy & Politics Institute, September 8, 2022, https://latino.ucla.edu/research/latina-care-work-covid19/.

CHAPTER 6

1. Eliza Haverstock, "'I Feel the Divine Feminine Rising'—Spanx Founder Sara Blakely on How Intuition Led to Her $1.2 Billion Blackstone Exit," *Forbes*, December 9, 2021, https://www.forbes.com/sites/elizahaverstock/2021/12/09/i-feel-the-divine-feminine-risingspanx-founder-sara-blakely-on-how-intuition-led-to-her-12-billion-blackstone-exit/.
2. Julia Boorstin, *When Women Lead: What They Achieve, Why They Succeed, and How We Can Learn from Them* (Avid Reader Press, 2022).
3. Niels Bosma et al., *Global Entrepreneurship Monitor, 2019/2020 Global Report*, Global Entrepreneurship Research Association, 2020, https://www.babson.edu/media/babson/assets/global-entrepreneurship-monitor/2019-2020-GEM-Global-Report.pdf.
4. Paul Sullivan, "Investing in Social Good Is Finally Becoming Profitable," *The New York Times*, August 28, 2020, https://www.nytimes.com/2020/08/28/your-money/impact-investing-coronavirus.html/.

CHAPTER 7

1. Andie Kramer, "Women Need Mentors Now More Than Ever," *Forbes*, July 14, 2021, https://www.forbes.com/sites/andiekramer/2021/07/14/women-need-mentors-now-more-than-ever.
2. Sylvia Ann Hewlett et al., "The Sponsor Effect: Breaking Through the Last Glass Ceiling," *Harvard Business Review*, December 2010, https://www.wearethecity.com/wp-content/uploads/2014/10/The-Sponsor-Effect.pdf.

3. Christopher "CJ" Gross, "A Better Approach to Mentorship," *Harvard Business Review*, June 6, 2023, https://hbr.org/2023/06/a-better-approach-to-mentorship/.
4. Christine Comaford, "76% of People Think Mentors Are Important, but Only 37% Have One," *Forbes*, July 3, 2019, https://www.forbes.com/sites/christinecomaford/2019/07/03/new-study-76-of-people-think-mentors-are-important-but-only-37-have-one/?sh=611571c64329.

CHAPTER 8

1. "What 'mother' means to Gen Z," ChatGPT, October 25, 2025. Compiled from multiple sources, including *Time* magazine (2023), *Them* magazine (2023), *Mamma Mia* (2023), and GoCo (2024).

CHAPTER 11

1. Sara Silano, "Women Founders Get 2% of Venture Capital Funding in U.S.," Morningstar, Inc., March 6, 2023, https://www.morningstar.com/alternative-investments/women-founders-get-2-venture-capital-funding-us.

ABOUT THE AUTHOR

Author photo by Gaby de Sarthe

ALEXIS MERUELO is a dynamic business leader, philanthropist, and advocate for women's empowerment, dedicated to helping others rise to their full potential—starting from within. As chief vision and purpose officer of the Meruelo Group, she leads Corporate Social Responsibility initiatives within the hospitality industry. Her mission is to use business as a force for good, embedding purpose and equity into every level of the organization while creating opportunities for underserved communities across Nevada and beyond.

In November 2025, Alexis launched The Business of Her, a women's leadership conference designed to equip women with the tools, connections, and confidence they need to lead in business and in life. Held at the SAHARA Las Vegas—the only Latino-owned casino on the Strip—the one-day event features transformative panels, skill-building workshops, high-impact networking, and a $10,000 business grant competition for local female entrepreneurs, along with additional cash grants for two runners-up. More than just a conference, The Business of Her is a movement to help women believe in themselves, claim their seat at the table, and build the careers and businesses they've always envisioned.

Building on this vision, Alexis coaches and mentors young women 1:1 to gain clarity on their next steps in their career. For more information and resources, you can sign up on her website: alexismeruelo.com. Drawing from her own journey—including overcoming imposter syndrome—Alexis mentors women to not only set bold goals but also take action and own their power.

A proud alumna of the University of Notre Dame, with both BBA and MBA degrees, Alexis serves on the boards of the Hospitality Charitable Foundation and the Notre Dame Institute for Latino Studies and was named a United States–Spain Council Young Leader in 2025.

If you're ready to rise in your own career, Alexis invites you to join her mission. Follow her on social media, LinkedIn and Instagram (@Alexismeruelo, @businessofher), to learn more about The Business of Her, her mentorship and coaching, and ways she can support you on your journey to power.

www.ingramcontent.com/pod-product-compliance
Lightning Source LLC
Chambersburg PA
CBHW020730080726
47818CB00040B/537

* 9 7 8 1 9 6 3 8 2 7 4 0 8 *